SPECIAL CAMPAIGN SERIES   *No.* 21

THE INVASION OF FRANCE
1814

THE INVASION OF FRANCE, 1814

By

Captain F. W. O. MAYCOCK, D.S.O.

AUTHOR OF "NAPOLEON'S EUROPEAN CAMPAIGNS"
"THE NAPOLEONIC CAMPAIGN OF 1805"
"MARLBOROUGH'S CAMPAIGNS"
ETC.

WITH SIX MAPS AND PLANS

The Naval & Military Press Ltd

Published by

The Naval & Military Press Ltd

Unit 5 Riverside, Brambleside
Bellbrook Industrial Estate
Uckfield, East Sussex
TN22 1QQ England

Tel: +44 (0)1825 749494

www.naval-military-press.com
www.nmarchive.com

Cover illustration:
The Campaign of France, 1814, by Ernest Meissonier

*In reprinting in facsimile from the original, any imperfections are inevitably reproduced
and the quality may fall short of modern type and cartographic standards.*

Print and page size has been increased over the original publications to accommodate the oversized maps.

PREFACE

IT is surely a most curious coincidence that the centenary of the overthrow of Napoleon's aggressive system of military despotism by the Allies should coincide with the outbreak of the most gigantic struggle in which Europe has ever been involved.

Then, as now, the immediate cause of the war was the attempt by one nation to dominate the neighbouring states by force of arms, regardless of justice or of treaty obligations. At the beginning of the nineteenth century Napoleon aimed at the complete subjugation of Europe and, thanks to his unrivalled genius and the fact that through force of circumstances France had become a " nation in arms " in the modern sense of the words, he achieved a temporary though most phenomenal success.

At first he was opposed by the comparatively small standing armies of the neighbouring states, the bulk of whose inhabitants took little interest and practically no part in the operations.

By degrees, however, the exactions of his soldiery roused the spirit of popular resistance in the countries which they had overrun, and the people themselves began to take part in the struggle.

Russia proved that even a gigantic army, led by one of the greatest commanders known to history, is powerless to crush the resistance of a nation whose ruler, army and people are united in an unwavering determination to make every sacrifice rather than lose their independence.

Germany then rose in revolt against her oppressors, and, thanks in a great measure to the self-sacrificing patriotism of her sons and daughters of all ranks and classes, Napoleon was forced to retreat across the Rhine.

However, so insatiable was his ambition and boundless his belief in his " star " that it was necessary for the Allies to invade France and hurl him from the throne before a lasting peace could be secured.

The five great powers at present engaged in the most stupendous conflict which the world has ever witnessed also took part in the struggle waged in the same theatre of operations, just a hundred years ago.

They were grouped very differently, however, but then, as now, England and Russia were allies, fighting in the cause of freedom against a ruthless military despotism. The British navy and the

Russian army were the principal causes of Napoleon's downfall, though the small force which we sent to the Peninsula covered itself with imperishable glory.

Surely it is a most auspicious augury that after the interval of a hundred years the same two great nations should again be allied in a life-and-death struggle against a military despotism every whit as ruthless as that of the great Napoleon. Our former foe has now become our staunch ally, and the gallant armies, who have proved each other's worth on many a hard-fought field, are now fighting shoulder to shoulder in the defence of France against the unprovoked attack of her implacable enemy.

Belgium once again has been unfortunate enough to become the theatre of operations and has suffered grievously for her courage in maintaining her neutrality against overwhelming odds, but her gallant army has already covered itself with glory and by its magnificent stand at Liège has given us an opportunity of coming into line with our allies, in time to take part in the opening battle of one of the most fateful wars in the history of mankind.

A nation which deliberately adopts a policy of aggression and regards forces as the only valid argument, finds itself with few friends and many enemies ; she may prosper for a time, but sooner or later her pride is humbled and she pays a bitter price for her arrogant disregard for the rights of her neighbours.

During the last five hundred years many nations have attempted to upset the balance of power and make themselves predominant in Europe, but history has a knack of repeating itself, and the result has always been a disastrous and humiliating failure.

It is well that it should be so, and it is interesting to note that Great Britain has always sided against the disturber of the peace of Europe and has almost invariably been successful in her efforts to uphold the rights of the weaker nations.

By her command of the sea, she exercises a grim and relentless pressure, which, though it may not be immediately apparent, eventually strangles her opponent, and this power has been enormously increased by the present interdependence of nations and the vast increase of commerce during the last hundred years.

F. W. O. M

ROYAL MILITARY COLLEGE,
CAMBERLEY,
1st September 1914.

TABLE OF CONTENTS

CHAPTER I
INTRODUCTORY

PAGE

CHAPTER II
THE INVASION OF FRANCE

CHAPTER III
NAPOLEON ASSUMES THE OFFENSIVE

CHAPTER IV
NAPOLEON ATTACKS BLÜCHER

xi

CHAPTER V

NAPOLEON ATTACKS SCHWARZENBERG

PAGE

CHAPTER VI

NAPOLEON'S SECOND ATTACK ON BLÜCHER

CHAPTER VII

NAPOLEON'S SECOND ATTACK ON SCHWARZENBERG

CHAPTER VIII
The Final Advance on Paris

CHAPTER IX
The Progress of the Campaign in the Subsidiary Theatres of War

APPENDIX
Detail of the Allied and French Forces at the Commencement of the Campaign

MAPS AND PLANS

THE INVASION OF FRANCE, 1814

CHAPTER I

INTRODUCTORY

Effects of the Disasters of the Previous Campaign—The Condition of France at the Beginning of 1814—The Country desires Peace—Napoleon's Preparations for the Defence of the Empire—Characters of Schwarzenberg, Blücher, the Czar and Metternich

To Napoleon, the year 1813 proved even more disastrous than its predecessor, for the campaign had ended in a crushing defeat at Leipzig, and though the transitory success gained over Wrede at Hanau had enabled the beaten army to cross the Rhine unmolested, the situation was none the less extremely critical. Hitherto invincible on the field of battle, the Emperor had been decisively defeated. France found herself forsaken by her allies, while the miserable remnant of the 300,000 conscripts hurried to the front some few months earlier, long before they had reached the legal age, were dying in thousands from typhus and dysentery.

A   I

Lying bulletins no longer availed to minimise the consternation caused by the long series of disasters, which had occurred in such close proximity to the frontier that the inhabitants of the Rhine provinces had tangible evidence of the severity of the reverses and of the forlorn state of the army. Had the Allies been able to follow up their successes in the field by a prompt and vigorous pursuit, they would have met with but little resistance ; however, the sudden overthrow of the French rule and the disruption of the " Confederation of the Rhine " had plunged the whole of Germany into such hopeless chaos that a considerable time must necessarily elapse before the confusion could be remedied. Moreover, political differences paralysed the strategy of the Allies, whose troops had also suffered heavy losses during the late campaign, while Prince Schwarzenberg, the nominal generalissimo of the armies of the Confederation, was utterly deficient of that " driving power " which is so marked a characteristic of the really great commander.

Thus it happened that the Emperor was allowed several precious weeks' respite before he was called upon to defend his frontiers, and he used the breathing-space afforded him by the difficulties and incompetence of his opponents to the best possible advantage. At the beginning of November the inhabitants of Mainz, long unused to the horrible realities of war, were appalled by the miserable state of the troops, some 70,000 strong, who for two days defiled continuously across the bridges over the Rhine. The town was filled to overflowing with thousands of sick, amongst whom typhus and dysentery wrought such havoc that for several weeks the death-rate reached the alarming proportion of over four hundred a day.

Though his presence was urgently needed in his capital, Napoleon was forced to remain with the army for some days to superintend the distribution of the troops along the left bank of the Rhine and to restore some semblance of discipline among the stricken host.

France, long a stranger to the stern realities of war, had now an opportunity of witnessing the price she paid for her triumphs and the misery wrought by the insatiable ambition of her ruler. Napoleon eventually arrived in Paris on the 9th of November, not in the least dismayed by his reverses, and fully determined to carry on the war, though the state of the country urgently demanded peace, if it could be obtained on any but the most ruinous terms.

On the 15th of November a fresh batch of 300,000 conscripts was called out, and though the legal age had been reduced to eighteen, and lads of seventeen were taken in thousands, recruits came in very slowly. The nation was horrified by the terrible sufferings endured by the troops during the last campaign; every vestige of enthusiasm had vanished. The price of a substitute had risen to between four and five hundred pounds, and even at that exorbitant sum it was almost impossible to find anyone willing to endure the hardships of military service. Recruits deserted in hundreds on their way to the depots, and to cope with this ever-increasing evil, the prefects were compelled to enforce the laws for the punishment of absconding conscripts with the most merciless severity. The bolder spirits, faced by the alternative of death on the field of battle or from disease, or of a rigorous imprisonment, naturally betook themselves to the mountains or forests, and thus increased the misery of the rural population by their depredations.

At a meeting of the Council of State, the Emperor explained the situation with the utmost frankness and set forth the measures he intended to adopt to deal with the desperate situation. He withdrew over a million pounds from the treasure hoarded in the vaults of the Tuileries, enormously increased the taxes on land, property of all sorts and salt, while the excise duties were nearly doubled, but even these drastic measures failed to produce the necessary supply of ready money. Three per cent. Government stock stood at forty-five, while the national credit had fallen so low that it was impossible to find a single capitalist willing to advance money on the State guarantee.

The Emperor's warlike policy met with no opposition from the Senate, but in the Chamber of Deputies, in spite of the fact that the President had been appointed by the Emperor and the vacant seats filled up by his nominees, a very different spirit prevailed. The session was opened by Napoleon with great pomp, and he delivered a stirring speech, in which he declared that the recent disasters were entirely due to the treachery of his allies, proclaimed his desire for peace, should suitable terms be offered, and concluded by calling on the deputies to shrink from no sacrifices necessary to ensure the safety of their native land. His oratory, however, produced very little effect, and it was obvious that a large proportion of the deputies desired peace on almost any terms and were bitterly opposed to the continuation of the struggle.

At the end of December, the report rendered on the terms offered by the Allied monarchs showed in most unmistakable manner the temper of the deputies, and in disgust the Emperor dissolved the

Chamber, and assumed the rôle of Dictator. The defences of the Empire urgently needed attention, and a commission had been ordered to investigate the state of the fortresses on the Belgian frontier and on the left bank of the Rhine. Their report, however, proved to be most discouraging, for France had been so long accustomed to wage offensive campaigns in distant countries that she had been lulled into a false state of security and had allowed the fortresses guarding her frontiers to fall into a lamentable state of disrepair.

Commissioners were also sent into the provinces to accelerate the despatch of conscripts to the various depots, collect supplies of arms and equipment and to arrange for a " levy *en masse* " of all the able-bodied inhabitants in the more exposed districts, in case of necessity. At the beginning of January 1814, an Imperial decree fixed the budget for the ensuing year at the enormous sum of £47,000,000 sterling, as it was then considered, but in spite of the large increase of taxation it appeared almost certain that a large proportion of this amount would remain uncollected.

The prodigious conscriptions of the two preceding years had ruined agriculture by withdrawing all the able-bodied men from the fields, while commerce had been almost destroyed by the undisputed command of the sea obtained by the British navy after Trafalgar.

The Emperor had of late years become more and more prone to deceive himself as to the possibilities of success, and had developed an almost fanatical belief in his " star." His faith, however, was by no means shared by his most able councillors; Caulaincourt urged him to accept the terms offered by the Allied sovereigns, and Talleyrand, his astute but unscrupulous Foreign Minister, was already busily intriguing with his enemies, fully convinced that the downfall of the Empire was inevitable.

Though the Emperor used every means in his power to rouse the spirit of national resistance and to make it appear that he was putting himself at the head of a united nation, determined to resist to the last the aggression of its enemies, he met with little success or encouragement. The Royalist, Clerical and Ultra-Republican parties, taking advantage of the popular discontent, commenced to intrigue actively against the Government, and though individually they could have effected little, their united efforts, combined with the profound discontent of the well-to-do classes and the sullen apathy of the people, added considerably to the difficulties and dangers of the situation. In fact, France was on the verge of absolute bankruptcy, and her resources, both of men and money, were almost exhausted by the ceaseless drain of the last two years.

One of the most immediate and pressing dangers was the continued success of operations of the Anglo-Spanish force under Wellington on the southern frontier, and Napoleon endeavoured to counteract this by offering to restore Ferdinand to the throne on the condition that he dismissed the British force from the Peninsula. He could not, however, make up his mind to withdraw his troops unreservedly from Spain, and consequently the Cortez eventually refused to ratify the agreement. His greatest difficulty, however, was the numerical weakness of the French forces and the fact that, except for the Guard and the troops serving under Soult and Suchet, the army was almost entirely composed of immature and partially trained conscripts.

After nearly twenty years of aggression, France once again found herself menaced by her foes on every side, as had been the case at the commencement of the revolutionary period, but the former energy and determination had been succeeded by a hopeless lethargy.

It has sometimes been urged that Napoleon jeopardised the success of the life-and-death struggle he was about to wage on the plains of Champagne against the main body of the Allies, by the number of troops he employed in the subsidiary theatres of operations, and thus violated his cardinal principle of massing superior numbers at the critical point. At first sight there appears some justification for this view, but on a closer consideration of the situation it becomes obvious that this dispersion was to a great extent unavoidable. When the Emperor had fallen back from the Elbe some three months previously, after the failure of his stroke at Blücher's army, a large number of French troops had been left as garrisons in Hamburg, Magdeburg, Dresden and some of the minor fortresses. Though, for the most part, they were young soldiers, taking part in their first campaign, they would have been veterans compared to the hastily raised regiments of conscripts with which Napoleon took the field in 1814. However, when the Emperor had concentrated to his rear, round Leipzig, to crush the main body of his opponents under Schwarzenberg, he had no intention of definitely abandoning the line of the Elbe and continuing his retreat to the Rhine. After disposing of his adversaries' main force, he had intended to resume the offensive, but the overwhelming reverse he met with in the great battle, and his subsequent hurried retreat, upset all his plans. Consequently large bodies of French troops, some 50,000 strong, composing the garrisons of the fortresses, were left to their fate in the midst of a hostile population and without any prospect of relief.

Owing to the great numerical superiority of his opponents, Napoleon had no option of assuming the offensive and was, for the first time in his career, compelled to embark on a defensive campaign.

Roughly, his plan was to contain the hostile forces in the subsidiary theatres by detachments, while he operated against the main armies of the Allies, under Schwarzenberg and Blücher, by means of two wings and a central reserve, under his own command. As he was too weak to defend the line of the Rhine, he entrusted Marmont with the rôle of observing and retarding the advance of the army of Silesia, while Mortier, Ney and Victor checked the progress of the Grand Army through the difficult country covered by the Vosges.

When the Allied forces had been somewhat reduced by the detachments necessary to observe the frontier fortresses and to safeguard their communications, Napoleon intended to join one of his wings with the picked force under his personal command and to fall on whichever of the hostile armies first offered him a favourable opportunity of striking a telling blow.

The knowledge of his opponents, gained in the previous campaign, convinced him that the hare and the tortoise might as reasonably be expected to run kindly in double harness as Blücher and Schwarzenberg co-operate successfully in carrying out any combined plan of operations.

Now that Massena, " the spoilt child of victory," undoubtedly by far the ablest of the French marshals, was living in retirement, broken in health and still in partial disgrace, owing to the failure of his campaign in the Peninsula against Wellington, the Emperor had only Soult on whom he could absolutely rely to carry out independent operations. The latter was a commander of remarkable ability, both as a strategist and a tactician, but was fully engaged in endeavouring to check Wellington's vigorous advance in the south of France. Suchet, Macdonald and Marmont, though not quite in the same class, were all commanders of outstanding ability ; the former especially had always proved himself a thoroughly capable leader in the field and was, moreover, an excellent administrator, but was by no means a favourite with Napoleon, principally on account of his incorruptible integrity and sternly republican principles. Macdonald, though capable, determined and singularly clear-headed, had never met with the success in the field to which his abilities undoubtedly entitled him, and was, as the Emperor said, " a most unfortunate general."

Marmont, a man of great intellectual power and a

brilliant strategist, was of a somewhat uncertain disposition and, as a tactician, was inclined to rashness, but was a most capable commander and a great favourite of the Emperor. Ney, brave as a lion and unrivalled at the art of covering the retreat of an army, was more remarkable for his extreme rashness on the field of battle than for his tactical ability. His intellect was not of a sufficiently high order to enable him to penetrate his opponent's designs or forecast his probable movements, hence as a strategist he was feeble and uncertain and quite out of his depth in command of an independent force.

Victor, Oudinot and Mortier were all excellent divisional commanders, who had won their bâtons by sheer hard fighting but were possessed of no exceptional ability, though they had all achieved considerable success in subordinate capacities. The Emperor expected little from his corps commanders but energy, coupled with prompt and unhesitating obedience; he was inclined to discourage initiative in his subordinates, hence, with few exceptions, the marshals were only at their best when serving under the immediate direction of their great chief. Moreover, most of them had amassed large fortunes during their numerous campaigns, and were weary of war; in fact, they longed for a period of peace in which to enjoy their hard-earned wealth. Napoleon was fully aware of their feelings and was consequently inclined to rely more and more on leaders such as Gerard, Morand and Maison, who had still their names to make and had not yet reached the summit of their ambitions.

Murat, who had returned to his kingdom of Naples at the close of the previous campaign, was actively intriguing with the Austrian Government, and was only restrained from throwing in his lot with the Allies by the fear of the restoration of the Bourbons to the throne of Naples. He wrote to Napoleon, suggesting that the whole of Italy, south of the Po, should be added to his dominions and guaranteeing in that case to hold it against the Austrians, but as he received no answer to his letter, he definitely decided to join the Allies.

The campaign of 1814 is often looked upon merely as an example of the advantages a really great commander can obtain from operating on interior lines against a numerically superior force and the masterly use the Emperor made of the network of rivers converging on Paris. But in reality the characters and aims of Blücher, Schwarzenberg, the Czar and Metternich exercised a far greater influence on the conduct of the campaign than the topography of the country or the fact that the Allies were operating on exterior lines, and explain many of the movements, which would otherwise appear almost incomprehensible.

The eventual success of the campaign was undoubtedly due in a great measure to the undaunted courage and grim determination of the veteran Prussian general, on whom the brunt of the fighting fell and who, in spite of difficulties and disasters, never for an instant abandoned his intention of advancing on the French capital. Though Blücher was seventy-two years of age, he had lost none of his pristine energy and but little of his youthful vigour, while the way in which he endured the strain and hardships of the campaign was truly marvellous. His career had been a most chequered one, for when little more than a boy, he had entered the Swedish service but had been shortly afterwards taken prisoner by the Prussians and joined one of their Hussar regiments. During the occupation of Poland, his vigorous methods had caused him to fall into disfavour with Frederick the Great. He had been passed over for promotion and eventually dismissed from the army.

He then married and settled down to farm his estate; at heart, however, he was always a soldier, and continually petitioned to be allowed to return to the army. Frederick the Great would have none of him, and it was not until that monarch's death, some sixteen years later, that Frederick William reinstated him in his old regiment with the seniority he would have held, had he never left the service. He was promoted Major-General in 1794, having already earned a great reputation as a most energetic and capable cavalry leader. He saw no further active service until the disastrous campaign of 1806, when he commanded the cavalry at the battle of Auerstadt and greatly distinguished himself during the retreat of part of the beaten army to Lübeck and by his gallant defence of the town against over-whelming numbers.

At the close of the campaign, every Prussian commander who had been forced to surrender was brought before a court martial, and Blücher was one of the very few senior officers who came through the ordeal with an unimpaired reputation and whose conduct was held to have been beyond reproach.

At the commencement of the campaign of 1813, he was appointed to the command of the Prussian forces, and his vigorous and determined operations were primarily responsible for the success of the Allies and their final victory at Leipzig. Though not, perhaps, a really great commander in the fullest sense of the word, he had nevertheless a remarkable genius for war and had an extraordinary gift for getting the most out of his troops, by whom he was trusted and beloved to an unusual degree. Inspired by his splendid courage and dogged determination to overcome every obstacle, they developed a remarkable power of endurance both on the march and on the field of battle.

Strangely enough, his great qualities were not fully recognised by the senior officers of the Prussian army, who, highly skilled in all that pertained to the theory of their profession, were inclined to look upon him as a brave but ignorant old man, who owed his selection for supreme command to his popularity with the army and the public. Müffling once wrote to the effect that everyone was aware that Blücher knew nothing about leading an army but simply approved the plans submitted him, and was so ignorant that he was incapable of understanding them or knowing whether they were good or bad.

He added that: " You can reckon on it that if he has given his word to engage in a common operation, that word will be kept even if the whole Prussian army be annihilated in the process." Loyalty, as was so clearly proved at Waterloo eighteen months later, was one of Blücher's most notable characteristics, and made him an invaluable ally to any commander who knew his own mind and was determined to carry through a preconceived plan of operations.

He undoubtedly owed much to the genius of Gneisenau, his singularly able chief of the staff, and was always most generous in acknowledging his indebtedness to his gifted subordinate; in fact, the latter probably received more than his due share of credit for the success obtained by his commander.

The usual procedure seems to have been for Gneisenau to submit an outline of the proposed operations to his chief, who, if he considered them suitable, carried them through with his own inimitable energy and determination.

But Blücher was no mere figure-head, whose every movement was controlled by the subtle brain of his chief of the staff; he was fully capable of originating a plan of campaign, while his power of rapidly coming to a decision and the vigour with which he carried out his projects were the principal factors of his success. At the critical periods of the campaign, his unshaken courage and the fact that, alone among the commanders of that period, he was not in the least disconcerted by the presence of Napoleon on the field of battle, were of immense value to the cause of the Allies.

The generalissimo of the Grand Army, Prince Schwarzenberg, was thirty years younger than his

B

confrère, the commander of the army of Silesia, and
a man of totally different temperament. He owed
his position much more to high birth and to political
considerations than to any remarkable military
capacity; in fact, though he had proved himself a
capable cavalry leader in a subordinate rôle, he was
more of a diplomatist than a soldier.

He had, however, seen a considerable amount of
service, having commanded a regiment of cuirassiers
in the campaign in Belgium in 1794, taken part in
the battle of Hohenlinden, served under Mack
during the operations round Ulm and been present
at Wagram. Napoleon had especially asked that
he should command the Austrian contingent, which
operated on the right flank of the " Grande Armée "
during the invasion of Russia, and he had afterwards
been selected to command the " Army of Bohemia,"
during the latter stages of the campaign of 1813.
He had also been Ambassador at the Court of the Czar
and had negotiated the marriage between Napoleon
and Marie Louise.

As a strategist, he was over-cautious and vacillating, belonging to the school of which Coburg and
Mack were such notable examples, and which considered that complicated manœuvres executed by a
number of separate columns and elaborate turning
movements, not decisive battles, were the main

objects of a campaign.   As a tactician he had proved himself singularly incapable of handling large bodies of troops on the field of battle, both at Dresden and at Leipzig, where his faulty dispositions almost involved the Allies in disaster on the first day of the battle.   It must, however, be admitted, in common justice, that his rôle had been an extremely difficult one, as he was hampered by the presence of the Allied monarchs and their train of diplomatists at his headquarters, and, moreover, the Austrian strategy was almost entirely subordinated to political considerations.   His partiality for gaining his object by manœuvring rather than by fighting was principally due to his singularly humane disposition, as he could not bear the idea of the losses even a successful action must entail.

A fine character, without the least personal ambition or craving for military fame, but with a considerable amount of tact and charm of manner, as a commander, Schwarzenberg was lamentably deficient in determination, while when opposed to Napoleon in person, his habitual caution degenerated into hopeless timidity.   The plan adopted by the Allies, during the second phase of the late campaign, of falling on the French detachments but avoiding a decisive engagement with the main body under the Emperor, had accentuated this failing until it had become a cardinal principle of the Austrian leader's strategy. His chief of the staff, Radetsky, a thoroughly capable and experienced soldier, unfortunately did not possess sufficient influence over his somewhat weak-willed commander to neutralise the evils caused by the subordination of military to political considerations.

The Czar, when once convinced that Napoleon's insatiable ambition was a perpetual menace to the peace of Europe, never wavered in his determination to continue the struggle until the latter's power for evil had been completely destroyed. Russia furnished far more than her share of the troops destined for the invasion of France, and this fact, coupled with his strength of character, gave the Czar's views great weight in the councils of the Allies, while his determination and singleness of purpose were of incalculable value to the common cause. Could all political jealousies have been temporarily laid aside and Alexander have assumed the supreme command of the Allied forces, the forthcoming operations in Champagne would have gained immensely in cohesion and vigour. The Czar's influence was constantly thwarted by Metternich, who, infinitely more anxious to further Austria's interests than to cripple the power of France, aimed at establishing a balance of power in Europe.

Unable to lay aside his jealousy of Russia and Prussia, whose interference with his designs for the partition of Poland he dreaded, he hoped that both his allies and France would be so weakened by the struggle that Austria would become the arbiter of the continent.

The readjustment of the existing frontiers, which must inevitably follow the conclusion of the campaign, would afford Austria a splendid opportunity for territorial aggrandisement, should she be in a position to take advantage of it. Consequently, Metternich intended that the Austrian army should take as little part as possible in the struggle, and that the great proportion of the losses should be borne by his allies. For his purpose the cautious Schwarzenberg was an ideal commander, as he was not in the least likely to run any unnecessary risk or jeopardise the safety of his army.

Though this selfish policy completely paralysed the strategy of the Allies, and seriously endangered the success of their operations, there was a certain amount of reason in the attitude Metternich adopted.

He had guided his country through a period of deadly peril with consummate skill, and the fact that Austria had retained her national existence was principally due to his patient diplomacy. Since the outbreak of the revolution, she had done far more

than any other nation to oppose French aggression
and had been forced to make great sacrifices during
the prolonged struggle, and though she had now
recovered to a great extent from her losses, she was
in no condition to risk another decisive reverse.

Therefore Metternich had no desire to adopt
extreme measures, but was, if possible, in favour
of settling the dispute by diplomacy rather than by
the arbitrament of the sword.

Napoleon, one of the most astute diplomatists of
his time, fully realised the inherent weakness of all
coalitions and had a very shrewd notion of the
divergent aims which paralysed his opponents'
strategy.

He also hoped that his father-in-law, the Emperor
of Austria, would be unwilling to proceed to ex-
tremities and thereby deprive his daughter of a
throne.

CHAPTER II

THE INVASION OF FRANCE

Difficulties of the Allies—Their Plan of Campaign—The Forces at their Disposal—The Passage of the Rhine—Distribution of the French Forces—The Advance of the Allies—Napoleon joins the Army

MEANWHILE the Czar had made a triumphant entry into Frankfort on the 5th of November and established his headquarters in the town, while Blücher's advanced troops pushed forward towards the Rhine. The small fortress of Hocheim which covered the bridge-head opposite Mainz was taken after some desultory skirmishing and the Allied troops then settled down into winter quarters. The army of Silesia went into cantonments between Coblentz and Mainz, while the bulk of the army of Bohemia was concentrated between the Main and the Neckar, though detachments were posted along the right bank of the Rhine as far south as Kehl.

As soon as the Allies had fixed their headquarters at Frankfort, an attempt was made to deal with the chaotic condition of Germany, caused by overthrow of the arrangements made during the French occupation. The Confederation of the Rhine, instituted

23

by Napoleon in 1806, had been dissolved immediately after the battle of Leipzig and a fresh league of the lesser German states had been formed.

A committee, presided over by Baron Stein, had assembled with the object of rectifying the frontiers, which had been altered by Napoleon in the most arbitrary manner. The most pressing and vital question, however, was the proportion of troops that each state should be called upon to supply, and the contingents were eventually fixed at double the numbers furnished during the existence of the " Confederation of the Rhine." Half were to be field troops and the remainder Landwehr, the latter being employed on garrison duty, on the lines of communications and in blockading the German fortresses still remaining in French hands.

The next step was to detach Switzerland from her dependence on France and to obtain permission for the passage of the Allied troops through Swiss territory. Denmark was also persuaded to abandon her alliance with France and to join the coalition, while a counter-revolution replaced the house of Orange on the throne of Holland.

Eventually Napoleon found himself confronted by a vast confederation, composed of Great Britain, Russia, Austria, Prussia, the smaller German states, Spain, Portugal, Sweden, Denmark and Holland.

Not even at the commencement of the Revolution had France been beset by such a formidable circle of foes, and under the circumstances, the offer of the Allied monarchs, that she should be confined to her natural boundaries, the Pyrenees, the Alps, the Rhine, was a most liberal one. Napoleon, however, could not bring himself to accept these generous terms, but hoping that some turn of fortune might once more carry his " eagles " to the Elbe or even the Vistula, he determined to carry on the struggle to the bitter end. He seemed totally unable to realise that an entirely new spirit had arisen in Europe, and that he could no longer hope to obtain recruits for his armies from the territories he might happen to occupy. Twenty years previously, hordes of ragged enthusiasts had swarmed over the neighbouring countries, proclaiming that they waged war only on the princes and rulers and had come to set the people free.

After a lengthy experience of the blessings of this so-called freedom, the inhabitants of the adjacent countries, exasperated by the rapacity and tyranny of their self-styled benefactors, had risen in their wrath and, forcing their rulers into action, had converged on the French frontier, determined to tear Napoleon from the throne and to put an end to his aggression.

The troops from the Germanic states, as well as those of Russia, Prussia and Austria, all had former humiliations to wipe out, or bitter wrongs to avenge, consequently the prospect of carrying the war into France aroused the greatest enthusiasm.

On the 1st of December, the Czar issued a proclamation setting forth that the Allies were not about to wage war against the French people but had only come to ensure their peace by driving Napoleon from the throne.

The decision to invade France had only been arrived at after considerable discussion and prolonged deliberation, for Bernadotte was bitterly opposed to the project and Metternich had no desire to take part in the movement. The Crown Prince of Sweden was so intensely vain, and his conduct was so entirely guided by self-interest, that his real views were always more or less of an enigma to his allies. He was supposed to harbour the ambition of succeeding Napoleon on the throne of France, should the latter be forced to abdicate, and at first the Czar was somewhat inclined to favour his pretensions, but the claims of the Bourbons proved too strong to be ignored, and there was, moreover, a considerable party in France desirous of their restoration.

Metternich then propounded a scheme, the leading feature of which was that the Grand Army should move through Switzerland to co-operate with Bellegarde in the subjugation of Northern Italy, while Bernadotte, advancing through Belgium, and Blücher, crossing the Rhine, combined in an invasion of France.

The Czar, naturally, refused to consent to a large force of Russian troops being employed in operations which could produce no decisive result and were undertaken for the sole purpose of regaining the Austrian possessions in Italy. His proposition, which, with some modifications, was eventually adopted, was based on a much more correct principle, and, in so far as it employed the whole available force of the coalition for a single well-defined object, was by no means a bad one. It had, however, several weak points, one of the most important being, that the advance took place on such an enormous front that a dangerous dispersion, at all events in the earlier stages of the movement, was inevitable and an accurately timed co-operation almost impossible.

Hence Napoleon would almost certainly be afforded an opportunity of falling on some isolated portion of the force and defeating the Allies in detail, more especially as two such dilatory commanders as Schwarzenberg and Bernadotte were allotted most important parts in the operations.

On paper, the Allies could dispose of a force of over a million men, but this included the Prussian Landwehr, engaged in blockading the French garrisons in Germany, and the Russian reserves, part of whom were still on the Vistula, while a large detachment were detained by the operations round Hamburg.

However, nearly 700,000 men might reasonably be reckoned on as available for operations in the field, and at the close of 1813 there were 150,000 Russians, 100,000 Austrians, 60,000 Prussians, 30,000 Bavarian and 12,000 Wurtemberg troops actually on the Rhine.[1]

The Allies proposed to put five distinct armies into the field: the Grand Army, composed of Austrians, Russians and Germans, under Schwarzenberg; the army of Silesia, consisting of Russians and Prussians, under Blücher; the army of the North, made up of Prussians, Russians, Germans and Swedes, under Bernadotte; an Austrian force, under Bellegarde, in Northern Italy; and the Anglo-Spanish army, under Wellington. There was, besides, a reserve army of Austrian, Russian and Prussian troops and detachments of British, Dutch and Danish troops destined to co-operate with Bernadotte in the Netherlands, as well as Murat's Neapolitans, who

[1] Horsetzky's " Chief Campaigns in Europe since 1792," p. 213.

might join the Austrian force in Italy. It was determined that the Grand Army should move southward through Switzerland, cross the Rhine above Basle and make for the gap between the Jura and Vosges mountains, in the neighbourhood of Belfort, and then advance through Burgundy to Langres, a town of considerable strategic importance, as it was the point on which several roads from the frontier converged.

By following this route, the Grand Army would avoid most of the fortresses guarding the Rhine, and also the difficult broken country covered by the Vosges. Its left wing, stretching southward, would threaten Eugene's communications through the Simplon and Mount Cenis passes, and it was hoped to induce him to abandon Italy, in which case Bellegarde could advance and, to a great extent, fill up the gap between the left of the Grand Army and the right of the Anglo-Spanish force. The army of Silesia was meanwhile to blockade Mainz, which contained a large French garrison, and only to commence its advance when the Grand Army had crossed the Rhine and penetrated some distance into France. While all this apparently endless discussion was taking place at the Allied head-quarters, Blücher was lashing himself into a state of furious impatience, for he alone seemed fully to realise the desperate plight of the French army, and the vital importance of crossing the Rhine and advancing on Paris before Napoleon had time to recruit his shattered forces and organise an effective resistance. However, every effort to spur head-quarters into immediate action was met by ex-aggerated reports of the strength of the hostile forces and specious arguments in favour of postponing any forward movement.

Instead of leading the advance across the Rhine, as he had hoped, Blücher, to his intense disgust, found himself charged with the blockade of Mainz, a duty not at all to the liking of the fiery field-marshal and one that could have been equally well performed by any of the subordinate generals.

Meanwhile Bernadotte had, as usual, done his best to paralyse the operations of his allies, for he had gone with the Swedish contingent to force the Danes to withdraw from the Norwegian territories. It was obvious that he would be unable to play his allotted part in the general forward movement and that the operations in the Netherlands would be left to Bulow and Winzingerode, while by his selfish disregard for the interests of the Alliance, the Crown Prince of Sweden ran a great risk of driving Denmark from the coalition.

However, at the end of the first week in December,

the Grand Army at last commenced its advance, and on the 21st, Schwarzenberg crossed the Rhine, with his centre at Basle and Laufenberg and his left at Schaffhausen.

The right wing, meanwhile, consisting of the corps of Wrede and Wittgenstein, had crossed the river at Fort Louis, some twenty miles below Strassburg, and had established itself in Alsace, to maintain communication between the army of Silesia and the Grand Army, while the latter carried out its extended circular march through Switzerland. The main body, under Schwarzenberg, made for the gap between the Jura and the Vosges, while the detachment under Count Bubna, on the extreme left, moved southward to Geneva, with the intention of operating in the valley of the Rhone and threatening Eugene's communications with France.

Blücher had the same force under his command with which he had achieved such decisive results in the preceding campaign, with the exception of Kleist's corps, which was engaged in blockading Erfurt and only joined him over a month after the advance had commenced. The Russian corps were commanded by Langeron and Sacken, the former being a complete nonentity, who consistently mismanaged any operations in which he took part, and was habitually inclined to thwart his leader's plans.

Sacken, however, was a man of very different character. Bold, resolute and energetic, he invariably carried out his orders to the letter, and was one of the hardest fighting generals in the Allied army. He was absolutely loyal to Blücher, to whom he was greatly attached, and throughout the campaign proved himself a thoroughly capable and reliable corps commander.

Yorck von Wartenberg, who commanded the Prussian corps, was a most capable soldier, who had greatly distinguished himself in the previous campaign, especially at the forcing of the Elbe, near the village of Wartenberg, whence he took his title, and later, during the fighting round Leipzig. Unfortunately, his great abilities were considerably discounted by his crabbed and contrary disposition, and, fully conscious of his own professional capabilities, he was embittered at not having been selected for supreme command. Touchy to a degree, and always prone to consider himself slighted, he seldom carried out his orders in their entirety unless they happened to coincide with his own views, and on several occasions his conduct had verged on the insubordinate. He never thoroughly appreciated Blücher's undoubted military ability, and was more often than not at variance with his chief, though on occasions a very real friendship existed between them. On the field of battle, however, he was brilliant, handling his men with exceptional ability and determination, but when once the actual fighting was over, he quickly relapsed into his habitual state of discontented obstruction. Blücher thoroughly appreciated his many excellent characteristics, always fully acknowledged his successes and invariably treated him with the greatest consideration, but Yorck could never be persuaded that he was not the victim of a clique of self-seeking generals of abilities far inferior to his own.

It was not until the 26th of December that Blücher, who had been chafing furiously at the delay, and had not even been able to complete the investment of Mainz, owing to the difficulty of bridging the river, which was full of floating ice, received the news that Schwarzenberg had at last crossed the Rhine, and that the hostile force consisted of only some 50,000 men widely distributed along the frontier. Blücher completed his plans with the utmost secrecy and, to throw the enemy off their guard, gave out that his force was to remain on the right bank of the river, and that he was about to establish his headquarters at Frankfort. To further mislead his opponents, he determined to cross the Rhine in three columns at widely separated points ; he himself, with Yorck's and Langeron's

c

corps, crossed at Kaub, half-way between Mainz and Coblentz, without experiencing any opposition, though the boats supporting the temporary bridge were several times carried away by the floating ice. Sacken crossed higher up the river, near Mannheim, but had first to capture a small redoubt on the opposite bank ; however, a strong party of Russian Light Infantry were sent across in boats, and had almost reached the opposite bank before they were discovered. The French garrison, some 300 strong, then opened a heavy fire, but successive parties of Russians were pushed across and the redoubt was captured at the fourth assault.

Meanwhile St Priest, with a strong Russian detachment, forced his way across the Rhine, lower down, opposite Coblentz, after a feeble resistance, and soon after daylight on the 1st of January 1814 the heads of the three columns composing the army of Silesia had successfully established themselves on the left bank. The crossing of the Rhine evoked the greatest enthusiasm among the troops, and Blücher was delighted with the complete triumph of his scheme, which had been carried out at the trifling cost of under 300 men.

In a letter to his wife, he sets forth his joy and pride in his achievement as follows :—" So long as the Rhine has gone by that name, no army of 80,000 men ever crossed it so cheaply; for I conquered thirteen cannon into the bargain and made 2000 prisoners." [1] Now that both armies had successfully established themselves on French territory, it remained to be seen whether they could carry out their somewhat risky programme without molestation. For the concentric advance of the Grand Army and the army of Silesia from such widely separated points, with the object of effecting their junction on the line Bar-sur-Aube-Joinville, in the heart of a hostile country, was indeed a most hazardous venture, especially when the opposing forces were directed by the genius of Napoleon. The danger was increased by the entirely opposite dispositions of the Allied commanders, for while Blücher was certain to push forward with the utmost vigour, regardless of every obstacle, it was equally certain that Schwarzenberg would seize every conceivable opportunity to suspend his advance and, even if he encountered no opposition, would move forward with the utmost deliberation.

The reasons for Schwarzenberg's circuitous march, though to a certain extent plausible, do not seem to have been of very great strategical importance; in fact, they were probably dictated by his own extreme caution and marked disinclination to run the least

[1] "Blücher," p. 203 (Heroes of Nations Series, E. F. Henderson).

risk, as well as Metternich's desire to postpone decisive action as long as possible.   Though by making
the lengthy detour through Switzerland the Grand
Army ensured the unopposed crossing of the Rhine
and turned the line of fortresses protecting the left
bank of the river, the Allies were so superior to the
scattered forces opposed to them that they could
have forced the passage at any point they chose,
with very little risk and small prospect of sustaining
serious loss.   Another argument advanced was that
by traversing the gap between the Vosges and the
Jura they would avoid the difficult country covered
by the former mountains and cross the larger rivers,
which generally flowed in a northerly or westerly
direction, near their sources.   Time, however, was
of vital consequence in the proposed operations,
though Blücher and Gneisenau alone of the senior
commanders seemed fully to recognise the fact, and
the prolonged delay caused by the inability of the Allies
to decide on a plan of campaign and by Schwarzenberg's unneccessary march, undoubtedly enabled
Napoleon to offer a much more effective resistance
than would otherwise have been possible.   The
difficulties of the terrain and of supplying a large
body of troops during their march through the
Palatinate and Lorraine, though serious, were by
no means insurmountable, as the advance of the

German armies, superior in numbers to Blücher and Schwarzenberg's combined forces, clearly proved some fifty years later.

At the end of the year 1813, Napoleon had, on paper, a force of about 250,000 men, not including garrison troops, to oppose the formidable forces menacing his frontiers, but of these 100,000 were in the south of France or in Spain and 50,000 in Italy, so that he had only about 100,000 men against the 350,000 under Schwarzenberg, Blücher, Bulow and Winzingerode, and of these less than two-thirds were actually on the frontier.

Five corps were distributed along the Rhine from below Düsseldorf to between Strassburg and Basle, to observe the Allied columns and retard their advance, disposed roughly as follows :—

Macdonald round Düsseldorf, with some 15,000 men ; Sebastiani near the junction of the Moselle with the Rhine, 5000 men ; Morand in the neighbourhood of Mainz, 15,000 men ; Marmont opposite Mannheim, 15,000 men ; Victor south of Strassburg, 13,000 men.

In the second line :

Maison in Belgium with nominally 20,000, but in reality about 10,000 men ; Mortier in the neighbourhood of Troyes, with part of the Guard and some other troops, not yet completely concentrated, about 18,000 men ; Ney, towards the southern extremity of the Vosges, with under 10,000 men.

Much farther to the south, a force under Augereau's command was to assemble round Lyons to keep up communication between the main army and the detached forces under Soult, Suchet and Eugene.

Though Napoleon was straining every nerve to reinforce his field troops, and filled up the ranks with almost untrained conscripts, many of the detachments were much under strength, notably those of Augereau and Maison.

There were, besides, a considerable number of troops, for the most part recruits with hardly any military training, serving as garrisons in the various frontier fortresses, ranging from nearly 15,000 in Mainz, 10,000 in Metz, Strassburg, Luxemburg and Antwerp, to 1500 in the smaller places, such as Saarlouis.

Not only had the Allies an enormous numerical superiority in the main theatre of operations but also their troops were of infinitely better quality, most of them, in fact, being veterans with at least one arduous campaign to their credit, while a considerable proportion of the French conscripts had received practically no military training, were most indifferently armed and almost entirely without equipment. In mounted troops and guns also the

Allies enjoyed nearly a fourfold superiority, and even though opposed by the greatest master of modern war, it seemed that nothing but a series of extraordinary blunders could possibly prevent their operations being crowned by a rapid and decisive triumph.

Napoleon, however, was not in the least dismayed by the heavy odds against him, but hoped that his opponents would be forced to detach such a large number of troops to safeguard their communications and to blockade the frontier fortresses that the balance in their favour would be very much reduced by the time they reached the Vosges and the Moselle, which formed his main line of defence.

After crossing the Rhine with his main body between Basle and Schaffhausen, Schwarzenberg wheeled to the right and advanced slowly, with his corps distributed on a broad front, while to protect his left, Count Bubna was ordered to move southward through Switzerland towards Geneva and subsequently to operate in the valley of the Rhone. On the opposite flank, meanwhile, Wrede (5th Corps) and Wittgenstein (6th Corps) advanced through Alsace, leaving detachments to observe Strassburg and Kehl, as well as the minor fortresses between the Vosges and the Rhine. The main body followed the high road from Basle to Paris, crossing the northern spurs of the Jura mountains and traversing the gap of Belfort, but merely observing the latter fortress, while De Tolly, with the reserve and the Russian and Prussian Guards, remained temporarily at Basle and invested Huningen. The Doubs was crossed at Montbeliard, and on the 10th of January, Schwarzenberg established his headquarters at Vesoul, the Allied columns having so far encountered practically no opposition. Unable to maintain his position in the Vosges in face of the formidable force arrayed against him, Victor, finding his right turned by the rapid advance of Wrede towards Neufchateau, abandoned Epinal after a sharp skirmish with Wurtemberg's corps.

Alarmed by his opponent's steady progress, Napoleon ordered Mortier to support Victor, but the former marshal was driven from Langres on the 17th, by Gyulai (3rd Corps) and again, attacked at Chaumont on the following day, was forced to continue his retreat. Schwarzenberg then established his headquarters in Langres, while Gyulai, Wrede and Wurtemberg continued to press Mortier back through Bar-sur-Aube and Vandœuvres to Troyes.

On the 25th of January Gyulai occupied Bar, with Wurtemberg on his right and Wrede, slightly in rear on the Marne, between Chaumont and Joinville, while farther to the north, Wittgenstein crossed the

Vosges and pushed forward towards Nancy without encountering any serious opposition.

Blücher, meanwhile, had pressed vigorously forward through the Palatinate, leaving Langeron with some 30,000 men to blockade Mainz, which contained a large French garrison, under Morand and St Priest on the Rhine to bring forward some reinforcements which had not yet reached the river.

In one of the principal squares of Coblentz, the Prefect had erected a monument recording the French occupation of Moscow and bearing the following inscription:—" To the great Napoleon, in honour of the immortal campaign of 1812." The Russian governor left the monument intact, but added beneath the original inscription: " Seen and approved by the Russian commander of Coblentz —1813 " [1]: a striking commentary on the sudden change in Napoleon's fortunes which had taken place since the disaster to his ill-fated expedition.

Finding himself too weak to oppose the army of Silesia, on the Rhine, Marmont, whose effective force was under 10,000 strong, fell back to Kaiserlautern on the 3rd of January, and then retiring across the Saar, blew up the bridges and took up a position near Saarlouis to check his opponent's advance.

Yorck and Sacken, however, concentrated their

[1] Alison's " History of Europe," vol. x., p. 85.

corps ; thereupon Marmont again retreated, halting for a short time at Metz, but eventually retiring southward towards Nancy in order to effect his junction with Ney and Victor.

Blücher wrote to Schwarzenberg on the 25th of January, to acquaint him with the situation, as follows : " To-day I arrived with the Silesian Army before Metz. Saarlouis and Landau are invested. Thionville and Luxemburg blockaded. I can give battle at the present moment with 74,000 men or on the 19th in front of Metz with 90,000 or later still with the number that your Highness knows." [1]

Two days later, he wrote to Rüchel : " The enemy had all his forces drawn up at Metz, but to-day I received the announcement that they had marched away to Verdun. So we are off to Paris. Unless we do something foolish we shall carry all before us. Marshal Schwarzenberg is a fine man, but he has three monarchs round him. Alexander is cleverer than any of his generals besides being the noblest of men." [2]

The fiery Prussian field-marshal had all along advocated a rapid advance on the French capital by both armies, based on the Rhine between Mainz

---

[1] " Blücher," pp. 204-205 (Heroes of the Nations Series, E. F. Henderson).

[2] *Ibid.*

and Strassburg; he was convinced that Napoleon would be unable to oppose the whole concentrated force of the Allies and that after one, or perhaps a couple of decisive battles, the French resistance would collapse and a lasting peace be assured by the occupation of Paris.

Yorck's corps was left to blockade Metz, which, though feebly garrisoned, was still a menace to the army's communications with the Rhine, while the Hessians were charged with the investment of Luxemburg and Thionville.

Thus Blücher's force was reduced to some 30,000 men, composed of Sacken's corps and a division of Langeron's corps, under Oolsofief, which had accompanied the main army. After a sharp skirmish on the 17th of January, Sacken drove Marmont from Nancy and occupied Toul two days later, then turning southward, he crossed the Marne at Joinville and advanced towards the Aube.

Blücher drove the weak French garrison from St Dizier, and leaving a detachment in the town, moved to his left to Brienne with Oolsofief's division, to effect his junction with the right wing of the Grand Army on the Aube. Gyulai had occupied Brienne a couple of days previously, but had moved forward to Bar, while Wittgenstein was some distance in rear and had not yet reached Joinville.

So far the plans of the Allies had been crowned with complete success, the passage of the Rhine had been effected almost without opposition, the difficult country covered by the Vosges and Jura mountains traversed and the Moselle and Meuse crossed ; in fact, the leading corps of the two armies were almost in touch between the Aube and the Marne.

Schwarzenberg, however, was already becoming anxious about his communications, though, as Blücher pointed out, any serious attempt against them by Napoleon would leave the road to Paris open to the Allies. The Austrian general, moreover, was by no means pleased to find that his energetic colleague had pushed his leading corps in front of the right wing of the Grand Army, instead of moving with his whole force concentrated and covering its right flank, as had been intended. A letter to his wife, in which he gave full vent to his feelings, showed that he also had fallen into the common delusion as to the relative position of the commander and chief of the staff of the Silesian army. " Blücher and still more Gneisenau, for the old fellow has to lend his name, are urging the march to Paris with perfectly childish rage. Without placing any considerable force on the road from Chalons to Nancy, they rush like mad to Brienne regardless of their flanks and rear." [1]

[1] " Blücher," p. 206 (Heroes of Nations Series, E. F. Henderson).

To such a cautious commander as Schwarzenberg, who regarded war as a formal game to be played in strict accordance with a number of elaborate rules, Blücher's headlong advance must have seemed rash to the verge of madness, and indeed the Austrian general had some grounds for his strictures.

The army of Silesia was now divided into three portions, the leading corps, under Blücher, being between the Aube and the Marne ; the next corps, under Yorck, was on the Moselle, and the third still on the march from the Rhine.   In fact, before many days had passed, the impetuous leader of the army of Silesia was only saved from what might have been serious disaster by one of those trivial accidents which so often exercise a vital influence on the fortunes of a campaign.

The Czar and Metternich had all along held totally divergent views on the question of dethroning Napoleon, and their differences had now reached such a pitch that they threatened seriously to jeopardise the success of the Allies' operations.   Eventually Metternich, who considered that sufficient advantages had already been obtained, and that the time had come for diplomacy to supersede strategy, declared that the Austrian troops should take no further part in the advance until a congress of ministers had been assembled to endeavour to arrive at a satisfactory settlement of the points at issue between Napoleon and the Allies.

The Czar retorted that he was absolutely determined to carry on the campaign alone, if necessary, while the King of Prussia refused to abandon the ally to whom he owed so much, though in his heart he was somewhat inclined to agree with the Austrian minister. Eventually, a compromise was agreed upon, a congress was to assemble at Chatillon at the beginning of February to meet the Emperor's plenipotentiary but the military operations were not to be suspended during its sitting.

At the commencement of the campaign, the French forces had been widely distributed along the left bank of the Rhine, from Düsseldorf to Basle, but they had drawn closer together as they had retired before the overwhelming strength developed by the Allies and were now disposed in two main groups, some forty miles apart. Mortier was on the eastern bank of the Seine, between Troyes and Arcis, while Marmont, Victor and Ney were on the Marne, in the neighbourhood of Chalons, whither Macdonald, who had been recalled from Belgium, after Winzingerode had crossed the Rhine, was also retreating.

While his troops were falling back from the frontier and concentrating on the line Chalons-Arcis-Troyes, Napoleon had remained in Paris, arranging for the government of the Empire during his absence at the front, organising a force for the defence of the capital and reviewing the conscripts on their way to reinforce the field armies. To deceive his opponents and encourage his own subjects, he caused the *Moniteur*, in its accounts of the functions, to give the totals at double and treble their actual strength.

The question of maintaining order in Paris itself caused the Emperor considerable uneasiness, for a certain amount of disaffection was already apparent, and this would naturally increase, should the Allies continue their advance. Consequently, he took considerable pains to organise a reliable National Guard under officers on whom he could implicitly rely, and entrusted the command to Marshal Moncey, who was also appointed military governor of the city. The regency was conferred on the Empress, with whom was associated his brother Joseph, formerly King of Spain, with the title of Lieutenant-General of the Empire. Berthier was sent on ahead to announce the Emperor's immediate arrival to the army, and at 3 A.M. on the 25th of January, Napoleon left Paris, accompanied by Count Bertrand, and reached Chalons, where the temporary headquarters had been established the same evening.

The raw French troops had suffered considerably in *moral* from the continual retreat during the

last three weeks; moreover, they were discouraged
by the inclement weather and numerous unsuccessful skirmishes against hopeless odds, but the arrival
of the Emperor immediately revived their drooping
spirits.

Napoleon spent the night of the 25th in receiving
reports from his generals regarding the positions of
his own and the opposing forces, and though he had
only some 65,000 men available, including Mortier's
detachment towards Troyes, he wisely determined
to strike at once, before his opponents became aware
of his proximity. Had Paris been strongly fortified
and an adequate garrison been available for its
defence, he was by no means unfavourably placed
for manœuvring against the enemy's flanks and
communications, but the necessity of preventing the
Allies approaching his capital cramped his strategy.
By moving to his left to gain touch with the Grand
Army, Blücher had exposed his main line of communications through Verdun and Metz to the Rhine
between Mainz and Mannheim, and he would have
been well advised to halt on the right bank of the
Meuse until he could have concentrated his whole
force, instead of pushing forward with only part of it.

The point of junction for the two armies had been
fixed too far westward, and Schwarzenberg's detour
to the left, to avoid the Vosges and turn the Meuse

and the Moselle had taken him too far to the south. It would probably have been much safer for the Allied armies to have effected their junction before crossing the Meuse, somewhere between Verdun and Neufchateau, though even then Schwarzenberg's communications through Langres would have been threatened by Mortier from Troyes.

Napoleon imagined that the army of Silesia was strung out along the road from Metz, and he consequently determined to fall on the flank of the leading columns of the Grand Army, between the Marne and the Aube, while Mortier attacked them from Troyes. He intended to move by Vitry-St Dizier-Joinville to Chaumont and leave Marmont, who would be shortly joined by Macdonald, at St Dizier to check any aggressive movement on Blücher's part.

On the morning of the 26th, Napoleon marched with some 35,000 men from Chalons to Vitry, continuing his advance next morning, and after a brush with some Cossacks, covering the front of the army of Silesia, drove the weak Russian detachment from St Dizier. He now learned that Blücher, with a slightly smaller force, was moving through Brienne to the Aube, and determined to fall upon him before he could effect his junction with the leading corps of Schwarzenberg's army.

D

CHAPTER III

NAPOLEON ASSUMES THE OFFENSIVE

The Actions at St Dizier and Brienne—The Battle of La Rothière
—The Allies fail to follow up their Victory—The Council
of War at Brienne—Schwarzenberg and Blücher to separate
—Marmont's successful Rearguard Action—Napoleon retreats to Troyes—Again Retreats to Nogent

NAPOLEON had now cut the army of Silesia in two,
and intending to follow up his success by attacking
Blücher in rear, he sent Marmont by the high road
through Joinville, while he himself, with Ney and
Victor, took the more westerly route by Vassy and
Montierender, through the difficult wooded country
covered by the forest of Der. The frost had broken
and the French army struggled painfully forward
along the country roads, knee-deep in mud, throughout the 28th, while the artillery would never have
got through the forest at all, had not the peasants
brought in their farm horses and even harnessed
themselves to the guns. However, on the 29th,
the weary troops debouched into the more open
country north-east of Brienne, where part of the
army of Silesia still lay, quite unconscious of the
proximity of their opponents.

Blücher was now in a most perilous position, for he was completely isolated, and had only Oolsofief's division of Langeron's corps actually with him, for he had sent Sacken towards Lesmont, on the Aube, to operate against Mortier and the bulk of his mounted troops had already crossed the river.

A lucky accident alone saved him from destruction, for a staff-officer bearing despatches ordering Mortier to co-operate in the attack on Brienne, and giving the positions of the French forces, was captured and brought before Blücher, who immediately despatched messengers to Sacken, ordering him to rejoin at once. Just before the attack developed, the Prussian commander was again favoured by a singular piece of good fortune, for Count Pahlen, at the head of the mounted troops belonging to Wittgenstein's corps of the Grand Army, appeared and at Blücher's request took up a position north-east of the town to check the French advance and cover the road by which Sacken would arrive.

The latter arrived during the course of the afternoon, after a rapid forced march, and passing safely in rear of Pahlen's dragoons, joined Oolsofief, who had drawn up his division immediately in front of the town.

The mounted troops then retired behind the Russian infantry, whereupon Napoleon, bringing up his numerous artillery, opened a destructive fire on the troops holding the outskirts of the town. The furious bombardment quickly set fire to a number of houses; while under cover of the smoke and confusion a strong column of French infantry, bursting into the suburbs, succeeded in capturing some Russian guns. Enfiladed by Sacken's batteries and furiously charged by the Russian cavalry, they were promptly driven out of the town, with the loss of some of their own guns, as well as of the captured pieces. The struggle raged fiercely but with varying success until long after darkness had fallen, when the French eventually drew off, leaving their opponents in undisputed possession of the town.

Blücher now imagined the battle over, and returning to the chateau of Brienne, which was situated on the highest point of the hill on which the town stood, ascended to the roof with Gneisenau to study the hostile position, clearly indicated by the lines of camp fires. The Russian outposts, however, performed their duties in a most perfunctory manner, for a strong force of French infantry suddenly burst into the grounds of the chateau and the Prussian leader and his chief of the staff barely escaped capture.

The hostile cavalry also charged into the town, and Blücher, who was watching the progress of the combat, was with difficulty persuaded to seek safety by the united efforts of his aide-de-camp, Nostitz and Gneisenau.

Sacken, who was issuing orders for the concentration of his corps, was almost ridden over by some squadrons of hostile cavalry galloping through the streets, but with great presence of mind backed his horse into a dark gateway and escaped observation. Blücher ordered Oolsofief to retake the chateau, but the French infantry were now firmly established in the grounds and fired with deadly effect on their assailants, who were clearly visible by the light of the blazing houses. Seeing that it was impossible to recapture the position, the Prussian leader drew off his troops about 2 A.M. on the morning of the 30th and commenced his retreat towards Bar.

On both sides the troops had been thrown into the fight as they arrived on the field, for Napoleon was forced to attack at once to hold his opponents to their position, while, in spite of a brilliant forced march, Sacken only arrived after the action had commenced. Consequently, neither leader had much chance of displaying his tactical ability, but Blücher's stroke, with the whole of the Russian cavalry, against the flank of Duhesme's division was singularly well timed and vigorously executed. The Prussian commander had looked upon the affair at St Dizier as an unimportant cavalry skirmish and it was only the fortunate capture of Berthier's despatch to Mortier that enlightened him as to the presence of Napoleon's formidable force in his immediate vicinity. Though the action had not commenced before 2 P.M., the casualties on either side amounted to about 3000, for the French had pressed home their attack with great vigour while the Russians had fought with their habitual obstinate courage.

Blücher did not continue his retreat very far, for Sacken halted a short distance south of La Rothière, while the remainder of the force took up its position just in rear, on the high ground in front of Trannes.

Schwarzenberg, who was at Chaumont, had also heard that Napoleon was at Vitry, and hastily sent out orders for the concentration of his scattered corps, while the Czar, who had only arrived that morning from Langres, instructed Barclay de Tolly, who was some distance in rear with the Russian Guard, to close up at once. Emboldened by the continual retreat and feeble opposition of their opponents, the Allied generals had carried out their advance somewhat carelessly and a rapid concentration was absolutely essential. Blücher still had some 27,000 men at Trannes but had completely lost touch with the remainder of his army, consequently, Schwarzenberg determined to join him with the corps composing the centre of the Grand Army and the Reserve.

Napoleon, who had not yet been joined by Marmont, took up his position some distance south of Brienne, across the road to Bar, with his right resting on the Aube at Dienville. He was by no means badly situated, for though, owing to unforeseen, circumstances, he had failed to destroy the force under Blücher, he was within easy communication of Macdonald at Chalons or Mortier between Troyes and Arcis, while he was connected with the latter marshal by Gerard's division at Piney. However, the Allies were steadily assembling a greatly superior force south of Trannes, and if he intended to strike, it behoved him to deliver his blow at once or to retire out of reach before he was overwhelmed by the masses of his opponents.

Under the circumstances it seems strange that he should have made no move during the 31st, but have remained quietly in his position, awaiting the arrival of Marmont. Meanwhile the Allies had been rapidly concentrating, and now had over 100,000 men in the neighbourhood of Trannes, for Schwarzenberg had brought up the corps of Gyulai and Wurtemberg as well as the Reserve, which included the Russian Guards, under de Tolly. Colloredo was west of the Aube, some ten miles on the road

towards Troyes, while Wrede was on the march from
Joinville to form the extreme right of the main body
and Wittgenstein was ordered to St Dizier to gain
touch with Yorck.

The fact that Napoleon made no attempt either
to attack or retreat on the 31st puzzled the Allies
considerably, and even led the Czar to doubt whether
the Emperor was present in person, but it was eventually determined to attack the French position next
morning. But as, from bitter experience, neither
the Russian or Prussian monarchs had the least
confidence in Schwarzenberg's generalship, he was
induced to hand over the command to Blücher,
though he still retained the disposal of the reserves
in his own hands and stipulated that, in the event
of a victory, Blücher should carry out the pursuit
towards Vitry, though it was most unlikely that the
French would retreat in that direction. Had
Schwarzenberg possessed the least ability, he could
have massed an overwhelming force against his
opponent, for Colloredo could have been ordered to
close up on the left bank of the Aube towards Dienville, Wittgenstein to act against the left and rear
of the French position and Yorck to threaten their
communications. Wrede's presence on the field,
which in reality decided the fate of the battle, was
entirely due to the Bavarian commander's own

initiative, as he had been intended to bear off to his right, to support Wittgenstein. It was decided that Gyulai, less one division left at Vandœuvres until the arrival of Colloredo, should advance against Dienville on both banks of the Aube, Sacken, supported by Oolsofief, against the hostile centre with Wurtemberg on the right, while Wrede would eventually come into action on the latter's outer flank.

Napoleon, who had under 50,000 men, a large proportion of whom were partially trained conscripts, and 130 guns, had originally no intention of fighting a decisive battle but had postponed his retreat owing to his uncertainty as to the course his opponents intended to adopt. Early on the morning of the 1st of February, Ney was ordered to march towards Lesmont to secure the bridge over the Aube, but a few hours later a careful reconnaisance convinced the Emperor that the Allies were already developing for a decisive attack and Ney was recalled. Gerard's corps occupied Dienville and extended on the right bank of the Aube towards La Rothière. Victor held the latter village as well as Petit Mesnil, Chaumesnil and La Giberie, while Marmont had now come into position on the extreme left, towards Morvilliers.

Ney's corps, on its return, would form the general

reserve, but at the commencement of the action only one of his divisions was available.

The cavalry was disposed in two groups under Grouchy and Nansouty respectively, the former between Petit Mesnil and Chaumesnil and the latter between the former village and La Rothière. Altogether the position was much too extensive for the force available, for, omitting the reserve under Ney, Napoleon had only some 35,000 men occupying a frontage of nearly seven miles.

The day was gloomy in the extreme and dense showers of snow periodically swept over the field, entirely blotting out every feature of the landscape, while partly on account of the inclement weather and partly on account of the confusion inseparable from divided command, the Allies did not advance to the attack until after one o'clock.

The Russian artillery commander had the greatest difficulty in bringing forward his guns, which sank to their axle-trees in the rain-sodden fields; eventually he was forced to double-horse half his batteries while he temporarily left the remainder in position on the high ground south of Trannes.

Meanwhile Gyulai advanced on both banks of the Aube against Dienville, Sacken against La Rothière, Wurtemberg on the wood in front of La Giberie, at the salient of the hostile position, while on his right,

Wrede, delayed by the state of the roads, eventually
came into action from the direction of Morvilliers.
Noting that the Russian infantry, ploughing their
way with difficulty across the sodden fields, had
fallen considerably behind their guns, Napoleon
ordered a strong body of cavalry to charge the
unprotected batteries. The veteran gunners, however,
who had just succeeded in coming into action under
a hot fire from the French artillery, were not in the
least disconcerted, but reserving their fire until the
hostile horsemen had approached to within five
hundred yards; they then opened such a rapid and
deadly fire that their assailants were driven from
the field with heavy loss. A blinding shower of
snow then temporarily put a stop to the hostilities, and during its continuance the Russian
commander seized the opportunity of sending back
his teams and bringing his remaining guns into action.

As soon as the snow cleared off, Sacken's infantry
advanced with magnificent steadiness against the
French centre round La Rothière, some of the
regiments even being played into action by their
bands.

The attack was pushed so fiercely that the leading
battalions reached the church of La Rothière, where
a desperate struggle ensued. Blinding showers of snow
again fell at intervals, and the men were often unable

to see to fire, but they nevertheless plied their bayonets with unremitting vigour.

A large body of Russian dragoons, advancing to support their comrades, then charged furiously, overthrowing the French cavalry and capturing twenty-eight guns in the centre of the hostile position.

Meanwhile the battle had raged with equal fury on either flank, though Gyulai's vigorous attack on Dienville had been beaten back with heavy loss.

On the opposite flank, however, Wurtemberg had driven the enemy's advanced troops from the wood in front of La Giberie, and making his way through the broken ground, intersected by ponds, had deployed on the open space in front of the village and commenced a vigorous attack. After a sharp struggle he drove his opponents from La Giberie and Petit Chaumesnil, but Napoleon sent forward a strong force of reserves, including part of the young Guard, while a large number of guns also supported the movement, and in the end the Allies were forced to abandon their position. Wrede, however, had now come into action on the extreme right, and as Wurtemberg again advanced, the superiority of numbers told its tale, and after a gallant resistance the French were forced to retreat and the Allies established themselves firmly in the two villages.

They had now gained possession of the salient of

the French position, and Wurtemberg captured a battery between La Giberie and La Rothière, then turning sharp to his left, he took the defenders of the latter village in flank and, aided by Sacken, drove them from their position. Wrede meanwhile had moved off to his right and, after a hard-fought struggle, had captured Chaumesnil and a battery of guns. It was now after six o'clock and the French left and centre had been completely routed, though the right still held its ground in Dienville in spite of Gyulai's vigorous efforts to capture the village.

Napoleon, however, was not the commander to give up a struggle while he had a reserve in hand, and bringing forward two divisions under Oudinot, which had not yet been engaged, he collected every available man and gun for a desperate effort against La Rothière. Blücher also collected his available reserves, as he had been quick to realise the meaning of the concentration in rear of the hostile centre. By the feeble light of the watery moon, the French advanced resolutely to the attack and cheering lustily drove their opponents from the village at the point of the bayonet, after a brief but desperate struggle. The Czar then sent forward some regiments of grenadiers, supported by part of the Guard, and after a furious combat among the houses and gardens, in which Duhesme's division was almost annihilated, the Allies at last regained possession of the village. During the confused mêlée, Napoleon had exposed himself recklessly in order to animate his wavering troops, while Blücher, as usual, had revelled in the thick of the fighting.

Seeing that it was impossible to retain his hold on La Rothière, Napoleon ordered the village to be set on fire, and drew off his shattered troops towards Brienne, under the cover of darkness, while Gerard was at last forced to abandon Dienville, and the whole position fell into the hands of the Allies.

Though the French troops had fought with great gallantry, especially under the eye of the Emperor, round La Rothière, they fell into a hopeless state of confusion during the retreat. Appalled by the slaughter, the conscripts, suffering severely from cold and hunger, and without the discipline which causes trained soldiers to stick instinctively to their corps, straggled over the countryside, casting away their arms and deserting in large numbers.

Fortunately, there had been no pursuit, as the battle had not been decided until long after dark, and the Allies, paralysed by the division of command between Blücher and Schwarzenberg, and ignorant of the country, had kept their formidable body of mounted troops in reserve, some considerable

distance in rear. Had they been launched at once on
the heels of the crowd of disorganised fugitives, the
French army must have been annihilated, but as it
was they reached Brienne unmolested. Expecting
every moment to hear the shouts of the pursuing
horsemen, the Emperor spent a most anxious time
in the chateau of Brienne, but as there was no sign
of the enemy, the weary fugitives went into bivouac
round the town, and towards morning he snatched
a few hours' rest. Though the action had been
commenced late in the day, and constantly interrupted by heavy falls of snow, the losses had been
by no means light, the Allies having some 4000
killed and wounded, while the French, including
prisoners, had lost about 6000 men and had, in addition, been forced to abandon nearly 70 guns. Next
morning the Emperor decided to cross the Aube at
Lesmont and retire to Troyes, the movement being
covered by Mortier on the left bank of the river and
Ney on the right, while Marmont, retreating northward to Rosny, held the line of the Voire. Through
a series of unforeseen accidents, Napoleon's brilliantly
conceived and boldly executed offensive had ended
in disaster, while he had lost 9000 of his best troops
and a large number of guns in the fierce fighting at
Brienne and La Rothière without achieving any
decisive result. The two hostile armies had effected

their junction, and he had been defeated by one of Blücher's and four of Schwarzenberg's corps, though he had brought the greater part of his field army into action. His decision to fight at La Rothière, considering the great superiority of the Allies, not only in numbers, but in the quality of their troops, seems difficult to justify. Even his position was a most faulty one, for he was hemmed in against the Aube, with only one line of retreat over the bridge at Lesmont, in rear of his right flank. Of course, a victory would have enormously heightened the *moral* of his troops, which had been seriously affected by continual retreat, but he could hardly have expected to achieve a decisive success against the greatly superior force opposed to him, even though it was commanded by such a feeble general as Schwarzenberg, and defeat might easily have entailed the destruction of his only available field army.

The explanation sometimes advanced, that he would have been unable to retreat across the Aube at Lesmont without fighting, does not seem very conclusive; for Schwarzenberg's movements were always so deliberate, while the outposts of the Grand Army were so unobservant and their reconnoitring so badly carried out, that it seems almost certain that Napoleon, operating in his own country, could have slipped away almost unmolested, had he wished to do so.

The Czar was delighted at the result of the battle and sent Blücher a message that he had crowned all his former victories by this glorious triumph.

In fact, with the possible exception of Gneisenau, who seems to have had a shrewd notion of the real situation, the Allied leaders were entirely carried away by their enthusiasm and, instead of organising a vigorous pursuit, wasted the day following the battle in feasting and mutual congratulations.

In reality, they had made little use of their opportunity, for Schwarzenberg had used only some 80,000 of the 125,000 men he had available, and Napoleon's army had numbered under 50,000. Neither Colloredo nor Wittgenstein had taken any part in the battle, though the former was at no great distance from the field, while the latter energetic and capable commander might easily have been instructed to act against the French rear, instead of being sent to gain touch with Yorck. On the actual field of battle, little use had been made of the enormous superiority of force possessed by the Allies; their strength had to a great extent been wasted in a purely frontal attack on the hostile position, and it was in reality only Wrede's advance from Morvilliers

E

against the extreme left of the French line, that decided the fate of the day.

The pursuit was carried out in such a half-hearted manner that touch with the main body of the defeated army was completely lost and it was imagined that Napoleon had retreated behind the Voire, whereas the only hostile force in that direction was Marmont's weak corps. The latter marshal, who had about 12,000 men under his command, was attacked by Wrede's corps, some 20,000 strong, during the afternoon of the 2nd of February, but he defended his position so skilfully that he was able to retreat during the evening, under cover of a heavy fall of snow, with very little loss. He then pursued his way unmolested to the Aube, which he crossed at Arcis, where he remained prepared to rejoin Napoleon or defend the line of the river, should the Allies attempt to cross at that point. At a council of war held at Brienne, it was eventually decided that the two armies should again separate, the ostensible reason being the difficulty of supplying such a large body of troops with food and forage if they remained concentrated, though probably the impossibility of any real co-operation between commanders of such entirely different temperaments as Blücher and Schwarzenberg had even more to do with the decision.

The actual plan approved by the council of war was : " That the Allied forces shall separate anew ; that the Silesian army of Field-Marshal Blücher shall at once march from here to Chalons, unite there with the scattered divisions of Generals Von Yorck, Von Kleist and Count Langeron, and then press on along the Marne past Meaux to Paris, while the main army turns towards Troyes, and likewise presses on to Paris along both banks of the Seine."

Having effected their junction, more by good fortune than by sound management, the Allies now deliberately separated and continued their advance on a double line of operations, thereby giving Napoleon a chance of attacking them in detail, an opportunity of which he was by no means slow to avail himself.

The chief physical features of the proposed theatre of operations were the rivers, which, running in a westerly direction, converged on Paris.

The Marne, the Aube, the Seine and the Yonne could only be passed by artillery at certain points, where permanent stone bridges existed, and these crossings had all been reconnoitred and prepared for defence, so that Napoleon was free to act on either bank of the rivers at pleasure, while the Allies would be forced to fight for every point of crossing during their advance.

A glance at Sketch Map No. 2 shows clearly at once the enormous importance of these rivers and explains the great effect they exercised on the ensuing operations.

Meanwhile Yorck, after a skirmish at St Dizier, had advanced to Chalons and driven a detachment of Macdonald's corps from the city, the French general, who was encumbered by a large convoy and the whole of Napoleon's reserve artillery, had thereupon retreated to Epernay and Chateau Thierry, following the main road to Paris, along the left bank of the Marne. Delighted at once more regaining his freedom of action, Blücher led Sacken's corps and Oolsofief's division through Rosny and St Ouen to Fere Champenoise. He then turned northward, sending Sacken towards Montmirail to co-operate with Yorck in the pursuit of Macdonald, while he moved to Bergeres to await the arrival of the reinforcements under Kleist.

The Grand Army, crossing the Aube at Bar, Dienville and Lesmont, moved slowly forward along the roads through Vandœuvres and Piney towards Troyes, while Wittgenstein advanced parallel to the general line of march but north of the Aube, to protect the right flank and keep up communication with Blücher.

Though he was at the head of a greatly superior

force and following up a defeated army, Schwarzenberg advanced with the greatest caution, much to the disgust of the Czar, who was eager to attack his opponents before they had time to recover from their reverse. Mortier had retired to Troyes immediately after the battle of La Rothière and had at once made preparations for defence, and though Napoleon had no intention of risking a decisive battle, he determined to remain for a few days in the town to reorganise his badly shaken army.

During the retreat nearly 6000 conscripts had thrown away their equipment and quietly returned to their homes, so that for the moment the Emperor had under 40,000 men actually with the colours.

Nevertheless he determined to put a bold face upon the matter, and convinced that Blücher would return to the Marne, he was firmly impressed with the idea that he had little to fear from the lethargic and cautious commander of the Grand Army. So feeble were the Allies' movements that Napoleon pushed forward a strong reconnaisance on the right bank of the Seine on the 5th of February and Schwarzenberg promptly fell back, withdrawing his headquarters to Bar. He then proposed to force Napoleon to abandon Troyes by sending the corps of Gyulai and Colloredo across the river above the town to seize the line of the Yonne and occupy Sens and Villeneuve. As it was evident that Schwarzenberg was not likely to afford him an opportunity of striking a decisive blow, and was about to have recourse to his favourite manœuvre, a wide turning movement, Napoleon determined to retreat. On the morning of the 6th, the French army abandoned Troyes and marched to Nogent, which they reached the following evening without molestation, while Marmont rejoined the main body from Arcis, where he had remained after his successful rearguard action.

Mortier, whose corps had remained behind to cover the retreat of the main body, did not attempt to defend Troyes, and the Allies, after taking elaborate precautions to avoid all pillage and destruction of private property, occupied the city on the 7th. The retreat to Nogent, though unavoidable from a military point of view, had exercised a most depressing effect on the spirits of the French troops, and no sooner had Napoleon arrived than he was greeted by fresh tidings of disaster : in Italy, Murat had at last definitely thrown in his lot with the Allies; Antwerp was besieged by a strong Anglo-Prussian force ; Maison had abandoned Flanders and was falling back to the frontier, while Blücher was rapidly advancing along the Marne. The cavalry had suffered such severe losses since the commencement of the campaign that it was reorganised into four weak corps under the command of Grouchy, while a new corps of infantry was formed under Oudinot, consisting of large bodies of conscripts from the interior of France, stiffened by the two veteran divisions, which were beginning to arrive from Spain. Caulaincourt also reported from Chatillon that the Allies, encouraged by their success, were increasing their demands, and now insisted that France should be limited to its original frontiers. Dismayed by these accumulated disasters, the Emperor's councillors urged him to accept peace on any terms, but though he instructed Caulaincourt to gain as much time as possible he absolutely declined to entertain the idea of restoring Antwerp.

CHAPTER IV

NAPOLEON ATTACKS BLÜCHER

The Emperor decides to attack the Army of Silesia—He marches
into the Valley of the Marne—Actions at Champaubert,
Montmirail, Chateau Thierry, Vauchamps—Blücher concentrates his Army round Chalons

FROM Chalons there are two roads running westward towards Paris, which unite again on the Marne
at La Ferte-sous-Jouarre. The northern road followed the left bank of the river through Epernay to
Chateau Thierry, where it crossed to the opposite
bank and then recrossed again at La Ferte-sous-
Jouarre. The southern road ran through Bergeres,
Etoges, Vauchamps, Montmirail to the Marne at La
Ferte-sous-Jouarre. These two roads form an elon-
gated oval, the maximum breadth of which is about
a dozen miles, while the distance from Chalons to
La Ferte is about forty miles by either route, though
the northern is the better. Blücher had never
actually effected his junction with Yorck, as the
latter was pursuing Macdonald along the northern
road, while Sacken was sent along the southern to
La Ferte-sous-Jouarre to endeavour to head off
the French marshal. Blücher himself, with the

headquarters of his army, remained near Vertus, while Oolsofief was stationed some little distance south of Champaubert to maintain touch with Wittgenstein, and Kleist with his Prussian corps, together with Kapzewitsch's division of Langeron's corps, were at Chalons, on their way to the front.

On the 6th of February, Blücher received a letter from Schwarzenberg, in which the latter stated that " Napoleon with the whole of his army was almost certainly still at Troyes." Without informing his colleague, the Austrian commander then withdrew Wittgenstein to take part in one of his dearly loved wide turning movements to manœuvre his opponent out of his position.

When he moved off, Wittgenstein had left a detachment, principally composed of mounted troops, under Seslawin, to keep touch with the left flank of the army of Silesia, but they were eventually withdrawn by Schwarzenberg to cover the right of the Grand Army. Blücher, however, knew nothing of these movements, and, imagining that Schwarzenberg was in close touch with Napoleon on the Seine, made no effort to rectify the dangerous dispersion of his corps.

Meanwhile Napoleon, seeing that there was no prospect of dealing an effective blow at any of the corps of the Grand Army, and receiving information of Blücher's rapid progress and the scattered position of his force, decided to overwhelm his most dangerous opponent before he could concentrate. The French reinforcements had already commenced to arrive, so that the Emperor was able to leave nearly 30,000 men on the Seine between Nogent and Bray, under Victor and Oudinot, to check the advance of the Grand Army and protect his capital.

On the 7th of February, Marmont, with the advance guard and the bulk of the artillery, left Nogent for Sezanne and was followed next day by Ney.

This apparently objectless march northward caused the greatest despondency amongst the troops, who were convinced that the Emperor had completely lost his head and was deliberately leaving the road to Paris open to the Allies.

The men were already suffering from hunger, and, to add to their misery, the road was so bad that it was almost impossible to drag the guns through the stiff clay, and Marmont, reporting that he was unable to proceed, gave orders to return to Nogent. The Emperor, however, had no intention of abandoning his carefully thought-out plan and ordered Marmont to push on, even if he were forced to leave his guns behind. However, by requisitioning the farm horses from the neighbouring districts to supplement his exhausted gun-teams, and aided by the indefatigable exertions of the peasants, the marshal eventually succeeded in getting his artillery and ammunition waggons to Sezanne.

The men had now got absolutely out of hand and, faced by imminent starvation, mercilessly pillaged the wretched inhabitants; in fact, the latter were so exasperated that the Emperor was forced to take vigorous measures to check the disorder, and issued the following proclamation :—" The Emperor has to express his displeasure to the army at the excesses to which it abandons itself. Such disorders are always hurtful : but they become criminal when committed in our native country. From this day forward, the chiefs of corps and the generals shall be held entirely responsible for them. The inhabitants are flying on every side, and the troops, instead of being their country's defenders, are becoming its scourge."

Napoleon himself left Nogent with the Guard on the morning of the 9th, and made such excellent progress that, in spite of the dreadful state of the road, he reached Sezanne the same evening.

Meanwhile Blücher was absolutely unconscious that his great opponent, with some 35,000 men, was almost within striking distance of the flank of the widely distributed army of Silesia. In spite of their

immense superiority in mounted troops, the reconnaisance carried out by the Grand Army had been
so futile that for two days touch had been completely
lost and Schwarzenberg was absolutely in the dark
as to his opponent's intentions. Imagining that
Napoleon intended to fight a decisive battle in the
vicinity of Nogent, he sent a message to Blücher,
begging for reinforcements, and the latter ordered
Oolsofief, Kleist and Kapzewitsch to march to his
colleague's assistance.

On the 9th of February, Yorck, with some 18,000
men, drove Macdonald across the Marne and occupied
Chateau Thierry. Sacken's corps, 20,000 strong,
was approaching La Ferte-sous-Jouarre, Kleist and
Kapzewitsch, also some 20,000 strong, were about
to march from Bergeres to Sezanne, while Oolsofief's
weak detachment of some 4000 Russians was still at
Champaubert.

Early on the morning of the 10th of February,
Marmont fell on the Russian outpost near the village
of Baye, taking them completely by surprise while
the men were cooking their breakfasts. Some of the
Cossacks managed to escape, and eventually reached
Sacken's corps, while the remainder hurriedly fell
back on the main body. Learning from a prisoner
captured during the skirmish that Napoleon was
present in person with a large force, Oolsofief sent

a courier to Blücher, reporting the fact, and asking for reinforcements.

The latter, unable to believe that the Emperor, with any considerable force, could have left Nogent unobserved by the Grand Army, imagined that his subordinate had only a small flying column to deal with, and as there were practically no troops available at headquarters, ordered the detachment to maintain its position. Meanwhile Oolsofief had drawn up his small force in front of Champaubert, and though he was aware that he was hopelessly outnumbered, prepared to hold his ground as long as possible.

Seeing with delight that the Russians intended to make a stand, Napoleon ordered his whole force to deploy, as he intended to make a frontal attack and envelop both his opponent's flanks. Two divisions, crossing the marsh in front of the left of the hostile position, drove in the small advanced post, while the cavalry, making a wide detour, reached the main road and threatened the enemy's right. As it was obviously impossible to hold the position in face of such an overwhelming superior force, Oolsofief left a brigade and a few guns in Champaubert to cover his retreat and endeavoured to make his way to Etoges with the remainder of the detachment. The rearguard held the village as long as possible, and, after a gallant defence, attempted to cut their way through their opponents but were surrounded and almost annihilated.

Meanwhile Oolsofief was forced to abandon most of his guns, as it was impossible to drag them through the mud, and finding his road to Etoges barred, endeavoured to fight his way through the fields to Montmirail, in hopes of being able to join Sacken. However, he was attacked on every side by overwhelming numbers, and his ammunition running short, he was eventually forced to surrender, though nearly 2000 men succeeded in cutting their way through their opponents and rejoining Blücher. The Russian casualties, including prisoners, amounted to over 2000 men, while the French losses were under 600 and they also captured 12 guns. This brilliant skirmish entirely restored the spirits of the French troops, who, always quick to appreciate the situation, immediately realised the importance of the action and the success which had attended the commencement of the Emperor's daring scheme. Though he could not believe that Napoleon himself had attacked his detachment, Blücher was seriously disturbed and determined to remedy the over-wide dispersion of his forces at once. A courier was sent to Sacken with an urgent message to march at once via Montmirail to Vertus. Yorck was ordered to join

him at the former village, while the previous instructions issued to the corps of Kleist and Kapzewitsch were cancelled and they were ordered to
march to Vertus. Blücher's efforts to concentrate
his army were, however, made too late, as Napoleon,
already on the Chalons-La Ferte-sous-Jouarre road,
had interposed between the scattered corps of the
Silesian army.

The Emperor lost no time in following up his advantage. Macdonald was ordered to halt at Meaux,
and next morning the main body marched to Montmirail to attack Sacken, while Marmont, with some
12,000 men, was sent to Etoges to contain Blücher.
Sacken received the order to return to Vertus on the
evening of the 10th, and set out next morning for
Montmirail, where he expected to pick up Yorck,
who, he was aware, had been ordered to join him at
that village. The latter, though he had received
his orders, which were reiterated next morning, did
not see any necessity for the proposed movement,
and remained at Chateau Thierry to repair the
bridge over the Marne, which had been destroyed
by Macdonald during his retreat.

On the morning of the 11th, the rival forces were
marching on Montmirail from Chateau Thierry and
Champaubert respectively, but the French reached
the village first and occupied it with their advanced

guard. Sacken then decided to take up a position west of the village and wait for Yorck, who, he expected, would come up on his left. He formed up his troops with his centre astride the main road, his right resting on the village of Marche, near the Morin rivulet, and his left on the open ground, north of the road, near Fontenelle.

Marching through Montmirail, the French troops deployed in succession west of the village, opposite the hostile position, and the action commenced soon after eleven o'clock. For some time the 40 guns drawn up in front of the Russian line checked the French advance, though south of the road a desperate struggle raged round Marche, which was taken and retaken on several occasions. Napoleon then slightly refused his left and made his serious attack on the opposite flank, so as to interpose between the Russians and Yorck's corps, which he expected to arrive from Chateau Thierry.

For some considerable time the French advance was checked by the accurate fire of the Russian skirmishers lining the hedges and occupying the farm buildings, but they were eventually driven back to the main position. A deadly struggle then commenced, both sides using the bayonet freely but without being able to gain any decisive advantage until Napoleon ordered the cuirassiers and Guard cavalry to charge. This proved the turning-point of the struggle, for the stubborn Russian infantry were at last thrown into disorder, while Ney and Mortier, converging on Greneaux, captured the farm buildings at the point of the bayonet and the whole left wing was driven in on the centre. After a dogged resistance the latter was also broken and the whole force attempted to make its way across the field towards Chateau Thierry, covered by repeated charges of the Russian cavalry. Late in the afternoon, after the fate of the battle had been decided, a couple of Prussian brigades at last arrived on the field, but they could only aid in covering the retreat of beaten troops. Twelve guns were abandoned, firmly fixed in the mud, and the remainder only dragged away with the greatest difficulty, while the Russian casualties amounted to considerably over 2000 men, of whom nearly a third were prisoners. Napoleon slept at Greneaux, well pleased with his victory, which had been won at the cost of under 1000 men killed and wounded, and at daybreak next morning took up the pursuit.

Ney, leading his horsemen with his wonted reckless gallantry, overthrew a body of Prussian cavalry, stationed across the road to check the pursuit, and then furiously assailed the retreating Russian infantry, which had barely time to form square. So

F

fiercely did he press his attack that two of the squares were broken and a number of prisoners, together with three guns, captured. Part of Yorck's corps now became involved in the struggle, but were thrown into disorder, and the Allies retreated in confusion across the Marne, breaking down bridges behind them. Both the Prussian and Russian troops had got completely out of hand and plundered the wretched inhabitants unmercifully during their hurried retreat through Chateau Thierry, in spite of every effort of their officers to check the disorder. The whole disaster was undoubtedly due to Yorck's flagrant disobedience of orders, for Sacken had confidently reckoned on his support at Montmirail, in which case the Allies would have been considerably superior to their opponents and would in all probability have driven them from their path. Napoleon had now succeeded in overthrowing the three detachments, which formed by far the larger half of the army of Silesia, and inflicted a loss of some 6000 men on his opponents at very little cost to himself. During the 13th of February, he remained at Chateau Thierry, giving his men a little sorely needed rest and superintending the repair of the bridges over the Marne.

Meanwhile Blücher, driven almost distracted by his inability to aid his corps commanders, had been forced to remain at Vertus, anxiously awaiting the return of Kleist and Kapzewitsch's corps. He sent an urgent appeal to Schwarzenberg to aid him, by operating vigorously against Napoleon's rear, but the Austrian general excused himself on the ground that the cross roads between the Seine and the Marne were impassable, and that it would be impossible to supply his troops during the march. He also suggested that Napoleon was merely manœuvring to gain time, and concluded by hoping that his colleague would have ample opportunity of concentrating his forces before he was seriously attacked. Blücher had been somewhat reassured by a pretended deserter, who reported that Napoleon, with the Guard, had returned to Paris, and as the return of Kleist and Kapzewitsch had brought up his force to some 17,000 men, including the remnants of Oolsofief's detachment, he determined to drive back Marmont and attack the main hostile force.

His natural optimism again asserted itself, and he wrote to his wife : " I have had three bitter days ; three times in three days Napoleon attacked me with all his forces, including his Guards ; but he has not attained his purpose and to-day is retreating to Paris. To-morrow I pursue him ; then both our armies unite and a battle before Paris will decide everything. Don't fear that we shall be beaten ;

that is out of the question unless unheard-of mistakes are made." [1]   However, his sanguine hopes were to be ruthlessly crushed, for, far from pursuing the French, the Prussian field-marshal was about to fall headlong into a carefully prepared trap.

As soon as Napoleon heard of his advance, he left Mortier to pursue Sacken and Yorck along the northern bank of the Marne, and marching from Chateau Thierry, on the evening of the 13th of February, reached Montmirail early the next morning.   Meanwhile Marmont had been attacked by Blücher and forced to abandon Etoges ; he conducted his retreat, however, with consummate skill, continually turning on his pursuers and forcing them to deploy but never becoming seriously engaged.   He halted at Vauchamps on the evening of the 13th, but was driven from the village next morning after a sharp skirmish.   He then retreated steadily along the road to Montmirail, drawing his opponents into the trap which the Emperor had prepared for them.

The Prussian advanced guard suddenly became aware of an increased resistance.   A large force of French cavalry appeared, followed by strong columns of infantry, while several fresh batteries came into action on either side of the road.   The Prussian vanguard was driven back in confusion and their

[1] " Blücher " (Heroes of the Nations Series, E. F. Henderson).

cuirassiers thrown into disorder by a fierce charge delivered by Grouchy, at head of a formidable force of cavalry. The Prussian infantry had barely time to form square before the hostile cavalry was upon them, and one of the squares was broken, but the remainder, firing with perfect steadiness and deadly effect, succeeded in beating off their opponents.

Realising that the opposing force was in overwhelming strength, Blücher saw that an immediate retreat was necessary, if a serious disaster was to be avoided. He promptly gave orders for the artillery to retire along the *chaussée* while the Russian and Prussian infantry, forming squares, marched through the fields on the right and left of the road respectively.

The country was flat and open, so that there was nothing to impede the free movement of the troops through the fields, though the ground was too soft to permit the artillery to move, except along the *chaussée*.

Napoleon had practically the whole of his cavalry available, and the formidable mass of French horsemen repeatedly tried to break the hostile squares. But the Russian and Prussian infantry, falling back with perfect steadiness, beat off every charge with deadly volleys of musketry, while the guns, unlimbering on the *chaussée*, came into action whenever

a favourable opportunity occurred.   Delighted with
the steadiness of his troops, Blücher ran great
risk of being captured, as he continually halted to
watch the admirable manner in which the Russian
infantry were conducting their retreat.

The latter, retiring as steadily as if they had
merely been carrying out a parade manœuvre, continually halted and fired with the greatest precision,
and the Prussian field-marshal, completely carried
away by his enthusiasm, repeatedly exclaimed : " See
how my brave Russians fight."

The French squadrons charged vigorously up to
the hedge of bayonets time after time, but could
make no impression on the veteran infantry, whose
steady volleys baffled their repeated onslaughts.
Champaubert was reached in safety, but the Allies
were delayed and somewhat disordered by the necessity of defiling through the narrow streets.   Napoleon
seized the opportunity, sending Grouchy, with the
better mounted half of the cavalry, by a detour
through the fields to cut off his opponents' retreat,
while the remaining squadrons furiously assailed
the hostile infantry, as the latter debouched into the
meadows, east of the village.   The Allies, however,
steadily forced their way towards Etoges, beyond
which village they would be comparatively safe,
as the country became so difficult that the French

cavalry could not act effectively. When they were within half-a-mile of their goal, however, they came upon Grouchy's squadrons drawn up across the road and a terrible disaster seemed inevitable.

Even Blücher was for a moment staggered by the desperate nature of the situation and halted outside one of the squares, determined not to survive the defeat. Nostitz, his aide-de-camp, remonstrated, saying: " If you should be killed here, do you really think history will praise you for it ? " Struck by the sound common-sense of the remark, Blücher determined to make one desperate effort to cut his way to safety, and ordered the colours to be unfurled and the drums to beat. Fortunately for the Allies, Grouchy's horse artillery had been unable to keep up with him, and was stuck fast in the mud some distance in rear. Advancing with the greatest gallantry, the hard-pressed infantry drove their way through their opponents, though the French cavalry, enraged at seeing their prey escape, charged furiously and succeeded in breaking some of the rearmost squares. A couple of Prussian regiments were captured and two Russian battalions cut to pieces, as, though escape was hopeless, they absolutely refused to surrender. The Russian horse artillery was completely surrounded but their commander promptly formed his men into line, and headed by

Blücher himself, sword in hand, they cut their way through the ranks of their opponents. Exhausted by their exertions, the Allies bivouacked round Etoges, but their troubles were by no means over, for during the night Marmont made a furious attack on the Russian brigade stationed at the western exit of the village, and a desperate struggle took place. He captured several guns, and fought his way into the village, throwing his opponents into a frightful state of confusion, but the Russian infantry quickly rallied and, using their bayonets with deadly effect, cleared their line of retreat and succeeded in reaching Bergeres soon after midnight. Here the exhausted troops obtained a little much-needed rest, and after order had been somewhat restored next morning, they continued their retreat to Chalons and went into bivouac on the right bank of the Marne on the evening of the 15th.

Seldom has a force extricated itself so successfully from such overwhelming difficulties, for the French troops, encouraged by their previous victories, pressed home their attacks with the greatest vigour and the country was singularly favourable for the action of their formidable force of mounted troops. The credit was due in equal measure to the promptness and determination of the leader and the unconquerable resolution of his veteran troops; in fact, the retreat from Vauchamps is undoubtedly one of Blücher's most brilliant exploits. Sir Hudson Lowe, who was attached to the headquarters of the army of Silesia, was most enthusiastic in his praise of the manner in which the movement was carried out, and wrote as follows :—

" I lack words to express my admiration of the intrepidity and discipline of the troops. The example of Field-Marshal Blücher himself, who was everywhere and in the most exposed situations, of Generals Kleist and Kapzewitsch, of General Gneisenau, who directed the movements of the *chaussée*, of General Zieten and Prince Augustine of Prussia, always at the head of his brigade, animating it to the most heroic efforts, could not fail to inspire the soldiers with a resolution that must even have struck the enemy with admiration and surprise." [1]

While Napoleon was engaged in vigorously pursuing Blücher, Mortier had driven back Yorck and Sacken, forcing them to retreat through Fismes and Reims, as there was no direct road from Chateau Thierry to Chalons along the northern bank of the Marne. Though Blücher and Gneisenau were fully aware that they had been heavily defeated, neither

---

[1] " Blücher," p. 224 (Heroes of the Nations Series, E. F. Henderson).

of them for an instant lost their courage, but, taking
prompt measures to restore the *moral* of their
troops, they resolutely minimised the severity of
the disaster. To Blücher himself, the events of the
last few days had been exceedingly bitter. Not only
had every one of the corps composing the army of
Silesia been decisively defeated but he had also lost
some 18,000 men and a number of guns, while his
reputation as a commander had been considerably
tarnished.

Fortunately his troops were composed of veterans,
devoted to their leader, and their faith in him was
much too firmly rooted to be shaken by any
temporary reverse, so that, as soon as the unavoidable confusion had been remedied, the spirit
of the army was as high as ever and they were
eager to once more try conclusions with their
foes.

Apart from the somewhat reckless dispersion of
his force, Blücher's reverses had resulted from a
variety of unforeseen causes, the most important of
which were undoubtedly Schwarzenberg's incapacity
and lethargy. The Prussian general had a right to
imagine that his colleague would at least keep him
informed as to Napoleon's movements and would
have communicated the fact that he had withdrawn not only Wittgenstein's corps but also the

detachment left by the latter general to maintain touch between the two armies.

Not only had Schwarzenberg omitted to do this but he had also completely lost contact with the main body of the hostile force and absolutely declined to make the least diversion in his colleague's favour, leaving him totally unsupported to bear the brunt of Napoleon's onslaught.

Yorck had also contributed materially to the disaster by his deliberate disobedience of orders and failure to co-operate with Sacken, but instead of realising his error, the Prussian general raged furiously against Blücher, to whose incapacity he most unjustly attributed the whole series of reverses.

Undoubtedly Napoleon had conceived and carried out his plans in his most masterly manner, for not only had he completely out-generalled his opponent but he had entirely retrieved his previous failure and had, moreover, achieved his success with very little loss. Not unnaturally, supposing that he had finally disposed of the army of Silesia, his spirits rose, and he once again saw himself carrying out a victorious campaign beyond the Rhine. He abandoned all idea of accepting the terms offered by the Allies and countermanded his previous instructions to Eugene to evacuate Italy and join Augereau.

CHAPTER V

NAPOLEON ATTACKS SCHWARZENBERG

The Cautious Advance of the Grand Army—The Allies cross the Seine—Marmont retreats—Alarm in Paris—Napoleon marches to support Marmont—Actions at Mormant—Nangis—Montereau—Schwarzenberg retreats to Troyes—Negotiations for an Armistice—Blücher marches from Chalons to the Seine—Schwarzenberg retreats across the Marne—The Corps of Bulow and Winzingerode placed under Blücher's Orders

AFTER wasting four days in Troyes, much to the Czar's annoyance, Schwarzenberg at last discovered that Napoleon had marched northward to attack Blücher, and, relieved by the absence of his dreaded opponent, issued orders for a general advance. On the 11th of February, the Prince of Wurtemberg captured Sens after a sharp skirmish, and on the same day Wrede's advanced guard, under Hardegg, drove the French into Nogent. Though he had only a small force at his disposal, General Bourmont made a most gallant resistance, but Nogent was stormed on the following day, and the garrison retreated across the Seine, after successfully destroying the bridge. Learning from the prisoners that Napoleon had taken practically his whole force with him, and

92

left only a weak screen of troops to hold the line of the Seine, Schwarzenberg made up his mind to act with a certain amount of vigour. On the morning of the 13th, Wurtemberg and the 1st Corps, temporarily commanded by Bianchi, as Colloredo had been wounded in the skirmishing that had taken place prior to the occupation of Troyes, crossed the river at Bray and Pont-sur-Seine respectively, and advanced towards Montreau and Provins. Victor and Oudinot were much too weak to resist the advance of the Allies and, sending their baggage ahead, fell back slowly towards Paris, skirmishing continually with their opponents' advanced troops.

South of the Seine the Allies met with practically no opposition, and their horsemen and light troops spread out on a broad front over the whole country between the Yonne and the Loire. Auxerre was taken by assault, Platoff occupied Montargis, after a slight skirmish, and the Cossacks pushed their patrols as far south as Orleans and west to Fontainebleau.

Schwarzenberg established his headquarters in Nogent and brought his reserves up to the southern bank of the Seine, between the latter town and Bray, while Wittgenstein pushed on towards Paris and Gyulai occupied the crossing over the Yonne. It almost seemed that Schwarzenberg would be compelled by the force of circumstances to occupy Paris, though he was by no means eager to do so, for it was obvious that Victor and Oudinot would be unable to resist the three corps which had already crossed the Seine.

The approach of the Allies caused the greatest consternation in the capital, as no adequate preparations for defence had been made, while the peasants in the districts between the Seine and the Loire were terrified by the Cossack patrols, which moved unmolested over the countryside.

Meanwhile Winzingerode's corps of Bernadotte's army had overrun Belgium and, crossing the frontier, had advanced to Laon, and on the 13th of February Chernicheff, with the advance guard, captured the important fortress of Soissons by a brilliant *coup de main*. The Russian commander hoped to gain touch with Blücher, whom he believed to be at Chateau Thierry, but learning of the series of disasters which had overtaken the army of Silesia, he rightly considered his position dangerously isolated and reluctantly determined to abandon the town, which was of considerable strategic importance, as it was situated on the Aisne at the junction of several important roads. The Russians then moved to their left, towards Reims, so as to be in a position to support the army of Silesia, which was assembling round Chalons.

Having disposed of Blücher, his most dangerous antagonist, Napoleon was now free to deal with Schwarzenberg, whose advance to within a couple of marches of Paris had caused the most profound alarm.

The Emperor had two courses open to him: he could either join Victor and Oudinot, who were with difficulty holding their position on the Yeres, or he could march via Sezanne to strike the flank rear of the Grand Army.

Strategically, the latter course would undoubtedly have been by far the most effective, as he would have severed his opponents' line of communications and driven them southward, away from their natural line of retreat through Troyes, Chaumont and Langres. By his junction with his marshals, he would simply force the hostile corps to concentrate and drive them back on their reserves, without threatening their line of retreat.

However, Paris was practically unfortified, and Victor and Oudinot, even though supported by Macdonald, who had already marched to their assistance, were too weak to maintain their position on the Yeres or to prevent the Allies occupying the capital, should they persist in their advance.

The fall of Paris would at once have ended Napoleon's dynasty, for the whole machinery of the government was centred in the capital, and its occupation would have been the signal for a formidable counter-revolution in favour of the Bourbons. Therefore political rather than military considerations decided the Emperor's plans, and on the 15th of February he marched with the Guard and cuirassiers to join the marshals on the Yeres.

Ney followed with the remainder of the force and the bulk of the artillery, while Marmont and Mortier were left to reoccupy Soissons and to observe Blücher and Winzingerode. Though the roads were in a terrible condition, Napoleon made a wonderful forced march through the difficult country covered by the forest of Brie, accomplishing 50 miles in two days and a night, and reached the Nogent-Paris road near Guinges on the evening of the 16th. Here he encountered a crowd of fugitives streaming towards Paris and the whole of the baggage belonging to Victor and Oudinot.

Napoleon realised that he had only just arrived in time; horses from the neighbouring villages were commandeered to supplement the exhausted gun-teams and waggons were turned about, their loads thrown out by the roadside and filled by Guard infantry, who were hurried forward to support their hard-pressed comrades. Victor and Oudinot's men were being steadily forced back, but had made a determined stand to cover the road from Meaux, by which Napoleon was expected to arrive. The timely reinforcement enabled them to check their opponents but, too exhausted for further effort, the weary infantry threw themselves down by the roadside to snatch a little much-needed rest. On the evening of the 16th, the various corps of the Grand Army were distributed as follows :—

Wittgenstein was at Nangis, with an advanced guard under Count Pahlen between Mormant and Guignes; Wrede was some few miles in rear, with his corps somewhat scattered, in the neighbourhood of Donnemarie; Wurtemberg was at Montereau; Bianchi was also in the neighbourhood of Montereau, with part of his corps on the left bank of the Seine towards Fontainebleau; Gyulai was farther to the south at Pont-sur-Yonne; the reserves were at Sens and between Bray and Nogent.

During the night, large reinforcements of veterans from Soult's army arrived at the French headquarters, Ney rejoined with the main body and the rest of the artillery, and by the morning of the 17th, Napoleon found himself at the head of nearly 50,000 men, a large proportion of whom were excellent troops. Pahlen now found himself in a most embarrassing position at Mormant. He had under 5000 men, a large proportion of whom were cavalry, and

G

a few guns, but he had received orders to remain in his present position, as the possibility of the arrival of Napoleon with a large force had not occurred to the Allied commanders. After spending the night under arms, momentarily expecting an attack, Pahlen commenced his retreat to Nangis on the morning of the 17th, with his infantry in squares and his cavalry on either flank. For two hours he fell back steadily, beating off the continual attacks of the French cavalry, but his own horsemen were eventually driven from the field and his guns captured, while the French horse artillery fired with deadly effect on his squares. Finally Milhaud's veteran cuirassiers, who had just arrived from Soult's army, charged home with irresistible vigour, and the stubborn Russian infantry was at last broken and driven in confusion along the road to Nangis.

Wittgenstein had hastened forward to support his advanced guard, but his men were thrown into disorder by the fugitives and the Russian general himself was within an ace of being captured. The route was now complete and the cuirassiers, pressing their pursuit with great vigour, captured over 2000 men and 11 guns. The Russians also lost about 900 killed and wounded, while two regiments suffered so heavily that they were struck off the muster rolls.

As soon as the French force reached Nangis, Oudinot was ordered to move on Nogent, Macdonald on Bray and Victor on Montereau, Napoleon being especially anxious to capture the latter town the same evening, as he would then be in a position to cut off the hostile corps on the Yonne.

He then fell on Wrede's corps, but the Guard and the cavalry were too exhausted by their forced march from the valley of the Marne to continue the pursuit, though Oudinot and Macdonald took a considerable number of prisoners. A Bavarian division took up its position on the heights of Valjouan, but it was promptly attacked by Gerard, while Bordesoulle's cavalry at the same time assailed it in rear. Retreating in disorder after a sharp skirmish, the Bavarians were only saved from destruction by the failure of L'Heritier to charge and lost heavily before they recrossed the Seine at Montereau.

Victor's men were too exhausted to attack the town on the evening of the 17th, and during the night the heights of Surville, which formed a natural bridge-head on the northern bank of the river, were occupied by the Prince of Wurtemberg, with the greater part of his corps and a strong force of artillery.

Bianchi also had a couple of Austrian divisions in support on the southern bank of the river, and altogether the Allies had some 18,000 men holding the town. Situated at the junction of the Seine and the Yonne, Montereau was a place of great strategic importance, and it was absolutely essential for the Allies to hold it as long as possible, so as to enable Bianchi's detachment at Fontainebleau to recross the Yonne. The strain was beginning to tell on Napoleon, who seemed totally unable to realise that though, inspired by his presence, his troops performed prodigies of endurance, there was a limit to their physical powers and that a reaction was bound to follow.

On the morning of the 18th, Victor attacked the heights of Surville, but was beaten back with heavy loss, while his son-in-law, General Chateau, a great favourite of the Emperor, was killed, as he was gallantly leading his grenadiers to the assault. Napoleon, who had been much annoyed by Victor's failure to seize the town on the previous evening, was furious at his want of success and immediately superseded him by Gerard. The latter attacked the position several times, but though he led his men with the greatest gallantry they were beaten back on every occasion by the steady volleys of the hostile infantry and the deadly fire of their artillery. It was now long past midday and Napoleon determined to use the whole of his available force to drive his stubborn opponents from their position; every gun of the reserve artillery was brought into action, while the Guard and the cuirassiers were brought forward to support Gerard, who was ordered to renew his attack.

Covered by the fire of 80 guns, 30,000 French troops advanced against the position, and Wurtemberg, realising that it was impossible to hold his ground in face of such enormous odds, gave orders for a retreat to the south bank of the river. His men commenced their retirement in excellent order, but the steepness of the slope and the necessity of defiling along a hollow road threw them into confusion, which was increased by the vigorous charges of the French horsemen. Napoleon hurried his artillery forward on to the captured heights, whence they played with deadly effect on the crowded ranks of his opponents, who were making for the bridge in the utmost confusion.

So eager was the Emperor to reap the full effect of his victory that he personally directed the fire of the Guard batteries, though the Austrian artillery on the opposite bank of the river was making excellent practice and their shots were falling fast amongst the French guns.

Wurtemberg strove gallantly to remedy the disorder and, thanks to his efforts, most of his corps crossed the river in safety, but the hostile cavalry and skirmishers pressed on vigorously and crossed the bridge at the heels of the fugitives, before they could fire the trains of the mines which had been already prepared. The Wurtembergers rallied on Bianchi's divisions but the French cavalry were followed by Duhesme's division at the double and after a sharp skirmish the Allies were driven out of the town, though not before they had succeeded in destroying the bridge over the Yonne.

In this desperately contested struggle both sides had lost heavily, the casualties on either side amounting to about 3000, mostly caused by the fire of artillery, for the French had lost heavily in their unsuccessful attacks on the heights, while the Wurtembergers had been punished severely during the retreat and had lost, in addition, nearly 2000 prisoners.

Napoleon watched the disorderly flight of his opponents with delight, exclaiming: " My heart is relieved, I have saved my capital."

On the evening of the 17th, Schwarzenberg had been informed of the disasters which had befallen the corps of Wittgenstein and Wrede and had immediately summoned a council of war, which was attended by the Czar and the King of Prussia, and it was decided to retreat at once towards Troyes and to summon Blücher from Chalons to join the Grand

Army. Late the same night a flag of truce was sent to the Emperor's headquarters, stating that the Allies were surprised at the resumption of the offensive by the French army as they had been about to sign an armistice, and suggesting a suspension of hostilities. After his brilliant successes against Blücher and his decisive victories over Wittgenstein and Wrede, the Emperor naturally refused to suspend his operations, and, as has been narrated above, defeated Wurtemberg and seized the bridge over the Seine at Montereau.

After the action, Victor approached Napoleon to protest against his supersession by Gerard, but was received with a torrent of invective. Nothing that the marshal could say in the least mitigated the Emperor's anger, and at last he exclaimed, in despair : " Victor has not forgotten his old occupation, I will shoulder a musket again, and take my place in the ranks of the Guard."

Napoleon, somewhat touched by his former companion's loyalty, gave him his hand, saying : " I cannot restore you to your corps, which I have given to Gerard, but you shall have a division of the Guard."

Victor was by no means the only senior officer to feel the weight of Napoleon's displeasure, for the Emperor bitterly reprimanded L'Heritier for his failure to charge at Nangis, Dejean for having allowed the artillery to run short of ammunition on the afternoon of the 18th, and Montbrun for having failed to prevent the Cossacks occupying Fontainebleau.

In the desperate situation in which he was placed, anything but the most decisive victories were useless to the Emperor, and his temper broke down badly under the strain; hence some of the reprimands he administered to his subordinates for want of energy were quite uncalled for.

After their defeat on the 17th, Wittgenstein had retreated by Provins to Nogent, while Wrede, with the greater part of his corps, had recrossed the Seine at Bray. Gyulai, Bianchi's detachment from Fontainebleau and the troops at Sens had also fallen back to join the main body, so that Schwarzenberg had practically the whole of his force concentrated in the neighbourhood of Nogent by the 19th. Though he was immensely superior to his opponent, the Austrian general decided to continue his retreat to Troyes, and the Grand Army retired unmolested and in excellent order during the 21st and 22nd, though a certain amount of confusion was caused on the latter day by the various columns converging towards their appointed rendezvous on the banks of the Seine.

Napoleon advanced to Nogent but made no attempt to pursue his opponents with vigour or to prevent the junction of their armies. His men were exhausted by their exertions and he spent some days at Nogent, reorganising his forces and vainly endeavouring to incite Augereau to act with energy against Schwarzenberg's communications.

Blücher, who had promptly reorganised his army, marched from Chalons by way of Arcis-sur-Aube to Mery-sur-Seine, with over 50,000 men, in excellent condition and full of fight, and reached the latter town on the 21st. The Allies had now over 180,000 men in position covering Troyes and as Napoleon had also advanced with between 60,000 and 70,000 men and drawn up his force some little distance from the Allies' position, a decisive battle seemed inevitable.

There was, however, a great difference in the spirit of the rival armies, for while the French were full of confidence and greatly encouraged by their recent victories, the Allies, somewhat shaken by the successive reverses they had sustained, were disheartened by Schwarzenberg's feeble leadership, which had resulted in their precipitate retreat before a vastly inferior force. The Austrian generalissimo was already meditating a further retirement to Langres and was confirmed in his intention by reports of some minor French successes on the Spanish frontier, in the valley of the Rhone and in the neighbourhood of Geneva.

Depression reigned at the headquarters of the Grand Army. The Austrian generals urged that their communications were seriously threatened, that the country was exhausted, that the army had lost heavily in the recent engagements and from disease —in fact, that the only rational course was to retire at once to gather reinforcements. Moreover, Augereau's force had been magnified by rumour until it reached the alarming total of over 40,000 men, while the main French army was supposed to number 180,000; in fact, everything seemed to indicate that a retreat to the Rhine was imminent.

However, Napoleon had as yet made no move and a reconnaisance in force by a formidable body of mounted troops was undertaken, which resulted in nothing more profitable than inaugurating a distant cannonade between the rival armies. On the 22nd, Bulow reported that he had arrived at Laon, and added that both he and Winzingerode, at Reims, had been placed in a dangerously isolated position by the march of the army of Silesia to the Seine.

On the same evening Schwarzenberg, alarmed by a report that Augereau was advancing from Lyons, took the bit between his teeth and ordered the Grand Army to prepare to retreat to Langres, while he ordered the first corps to march towards Dijon to safeguard his communications.

The Czar was greatly annoyed that the retrograde movement had been decided on without his consent, and Blücher raged furiously at his colleague's timidity, even offering to attack the hostile position with his own force if he was assured of the support of the Grand Army.

However, in spite of the opposition of the Czar, Frederick William and Blücher, Schwarzenberg remained unshaken and the Grand Army commenced to evacuate its position on the 23rd and abandoned Troyes on the following day, while the army of Silesia had perforce to comply with the movement and retreated towards the Aube.

Napoleon entered Troyes in triumph, receiving a great ovation from the inhabitants, who were overjoyed at their entirely unexpected deliverance from the presence of the Allies. Unfortunately his entry was stained by an act of needless cruelty, for in spite of the entreaties of his family and several of the principal inhabitants, he ordered the execution of M. Goualt, a prominent Royalist, who had declared for the Bourbons during the occupation of the city by the Allies.

Though the Grand Army had withdrawn from its position before Troyes unmolested, except for a slight skirmish between the rearguard under Wrede and the French advanced troops, a certain amount of unavoidable confusion arose during the march to the Aube, and it was therefore deemed advisable to endeavour to arrange an armistice. Napoleon agreed, but naturally refused to suspend hostilities during the conference, which was to assemble at Lusigny, and the Marne, as far north as Chalons, was agreed upon as the line of demarcation between the rival armies, while it was also stipulated that the Allies should be left in undisturbed possession of the passes through the Vosges. The Grand Army crossed the Aube unmolested, and took up a position round Colombey, midway between the latter river and the Marne, while its leader endeavoured to decide on some plan of operations.

On the 25th, a momentous council of war took place at Bar-sur-Aube, at which the Allied sovereigns, their ministers and Schwarzenberg, were present.

The Czar was most anxious to resume the offensive at the earliest possible moment and proposed that, as Bernadotte evidently had no intention of carrying out a vigorous campaign in Belgium, the two powerful corps of Bulow and Winzingerode should be transferred from the army of the north and placed under Blücher's command. It was pointed out that the Crown Prince of Sweden would bitterly resent this arrangement unless his sanction had been previously obtained, and as he was still on the Lower Rhine there seemed no prospect of obtaining his consent without a delay which would probably prove fatal to the proposed scheme. The Czar then suggested joining Blücher with the Russian Guard and Wittgenstein's corps and advancing on Paris, while the King of Prussia agreed to accompany him. This plan was, however, promptly vetoed, as the withdrawal of the Russian contingent would have seriously weakened the Grand Army and have led to Schwarzenberg's precipitate retreat to the Rhine.

At this critical moment, the British representative, Lord Castlereagh, intervened in the discussion and inquired if the junction of the corps of Bulow and Winzingerode with the army of Silesia was a military necessity.

The senior officers present unanimously agreed that this was the case, whereupon Lord Castlereagh insisted that the necessary orders should at once be given, and guaranteed to bring Bernadotte to reason, by stopping his monthly subsidy, if no other means would suffice.

As Great Britain was virtually the paymaster of

the coalition and her subsidies alone enabled the Allies to keep the field, Castlereagh's ultimatum, backed by the Czar's hearty approval, finally settled the question, and it was decided to place the corps of Bulow and Winzingerode under Blücher's command, thus giving him a formidable force of well over 100,000 men.

He was then to assume a vigorous offensive, drive back the hostile left under Marmont and advance on Paris, while the Grand Army was to fall back towards Langres, collect its reserves and manoeuvre against Napoleon, so as to retain as large a portion of his force as possible on the Upper Seine.

This arrangement, though it had the obvious disadvantage of dividing the Allied forces into two independent armies, gave Blücher a free hand and enabled him to carry out his operations unfettered by his vacillating colleague.

That the Prussian commander had a very sound appreciation of the situation was shown by the hasty outline of his plans, which he forwarded to the Czar. He pointed out that a general retreat would cause the whole country to take up arms, strengthen Napoleon's hands enormously and entail the most serious consequences to the inhabitants who had declared for the Bourbons; that the Allied troops would be disheartened and forced to retreat through districts in which the supplies had already been exhausted; while, on the other hand, if Bulow and Winzingerode were placed unreservedly under his command, he would be able to advance on Paris, regardless of any force that could be collected to oppose him,

Of late years, Napoleon had become increasingly apt to view the military situation more in accordance with his wishes than was warranted by the actual facts, and he now entirely overestimated the effect produced by his operations against the Grand Army. He imagined that Schwarzenberg was retreating in disorder towards Langres and that Blücher was endeavouring to join him by marching up the right bank of the Aube.

Consequently Gerard, supported by Ney and Oudinot, was ordered to pursue the Allies along the main road to Bar-sur-Aube, through Vandœuvres, while Macdonald, accompanied by a strong force of cavalry, was to follow the road along the left bank of the Seine towards Chatillon.

The remainder of the army was to concentrate round Troyes, while Marmont was to advance through Sezanne to menace Blücher's communications with Chalons, should the latter decide to break northward. The report that the army of Silesia was moving down the Aube, towards its junction with the Seine, by no means squared with Napoleon's ideas as to Blücher's probable movements, and he remained at Troyes, awaiting definite information from Marmont and Bordessoulle, who had been sent to Anglure to gain touch with the Prussians. It was possible that Blücher might not intend to join Schwarzenberg, but he was meditating a retreat to Chalons or even an advance on Paris, either by Sezanne and Meaux or through Nogent, and it was necessary to guard against either alternative.

Napoleon invariably issued his orders during the small hours of the morning; thus he was able to snatch a few hours' rest whilst the reports received during the previous evening were collected and compared. As no definite information had been received from either Marmont or Bordessoulle, the situation was still obscure; but if Blücher meditated an immediate advance on Paris he would encounter Marmont's detachment if he followed the road through Sezanne, or Arrighi's division at Nogent if he followed the right bank of the Seine. The Emperor himself was inclined to believe that the army of Silesia would move up the Aube towards Bar, to gain touch with the main body of the Grand Army; hence soon after 4 A.M. on the 25th, Ney was ordered to proceed to Arcis, while Victor was to return to Mery, to endeavour to ascertain what had become of the Prussians. Macdonald and Oudinot were ordered to continue their pursuit of the hostile columns towards Bar-sur-Aube and Chatillon respectively.

It is interesting to note that though Napoleon was generally able to forecast Schwarzenberg's movements with considerable accuracy, he seldom gauged Blücher's intentions correctly, for he persistently underrated the latter general's determined courage and sound grasp of the military situation.

CHAPTER VI

NAPOLEON'S SECOND ATTACK ON BLÜCHER

The Army of Silesia returns to the Marne—Napoleon follows Blücher—Capture of Soissons—Blücher crosses the Aisne and effects his Junction with Bulow and Winzingerode—Napoleon crosses the Aisne—The Battle of Craone—The Battle of Laon—Yorck's Successful Night Attack upon Marmont—Blücher's Illness—Gneisenau remains on the Defensive—Napoleon recaptures Reims

BLÜCHER, who had reorganised his scattered forces with wonderful rapidity, had marched from Chalons to the Seine, believing that Schwarzenberg had at last made up his mind to fight a pitched battle, which would decide the fate of the campaign, but, much to his disgust, he found that his colleague was determined to continue his retreat. No sooner was the fiery Prussian marshal informed that the corps of Bulow and Winzingerode had been placed under his command than he issued orders for an advance towards Meaux, intending to pick up his reinforcements on the way and push on to Paris.

Schwarzenberg, however, was again becoming nervous, and wrote suggesting that the army of Silesia should join him, holding out the prospect of a pitched battle in the neighbourhood of Colombey, midway between Bar and Chaumont.

Blücher had, however, advanced along the right bank of the Aube, breaking down the bridges at Arcis and Plancy, and replied by pointing out the impossibility of rejoining the Grand Army. He wrote: " In the course of last night I received your Grace's honoured communications of the morning and evening of the 24th, and perceive to my regret that there must be a misunderstanding or that a dispatch must have been lost. I have acted in accordance with the oral agreement which Colonel von Grolmann brought me. Yesterday my vanguard drove the enemy as far as La Ferte Gaucher and is drawn up in front of that position. Were I to turn back, I could under no circumstances effect my junction with your Grace within the stated time and should expose my army to the gravest perils. By moving on Paris, on the other hand, and operating in the rear of the Emperor Napoleon, I hope to secure for your Grace the most effectual relief." [1] The enemy he referred to was Marmont's detachment, which had advanced to Sezanne but had been forced to fall back by the advanced troops of the army of Silesia.

[1] " Blücher," p. 232 (Heroes of the Nations Series, E. F. Henderson).

Blücher also received dispatches from the King of Prussia and the Czar, the former informing him that the expected truce had not been ratified and that Schwarzenberg intended to continue his retreat, so that now everything depended on the army of Silesia, while the latter urged him to carry out a very vigorous offensive against the left wing of the hostile force.

Blücher, however, needed no exhortations to spur him to action, for he was already advancing rapidly along the road from Sezanne to the Marne at La Ferte-sous-Jouarre, with his cavalry covering his front and left bank, towards the main road from Nogent to Paris.

Marmont meanwhile had written to Mortier, suggesting that the latter should move to La Ferte-sous-Jouarre, where their forces could unite and they would then have some 10,000 men available to retard the Prussian advance.

In spite of the reports received from Marmont and Bordessoulle, Napoleon could not bring himself to believe that Blücher had commenced his advance on Paris, but was inclined to think that the army of Silesia was making for Chalons. However, it was obviously dangerous to allow the Prussian leader to carry out his plans unmolested, consequently Marmont and Mortier were to bar his advance westward, while Arrighi and Bordessoulle operated against his left and Ney, supported by Victor, was to cross the Aube, fall on his rear and cut him off from Chalons. On the evening of the 26th, the Emperor learned that Marmont had been forced to retreat towards Meaux, and he determined to set out with the Guard in pursuit of Blücher, leaving some 40,000 men under Macdonald to contain Schwarzenberg. The latter marshal was ordered to take up his position behind the Aube, hold Bar with a strong rearguard and destroy the bridges over the river, should the Grand Army show a disposition to assume a vigorous offensive. The Emperor hoped to drive his opponent against the Marne and, including the detachments under Marmont, Mortier, Arrighi and Bordessoulle, he would have about 50,000 men available to carry out his design.

He expected to be at Fere Champenoise with some 35,000 men early on the morning of the 28th, and he intended to follow Blücher through Sezanne, being joined at the latter village by Arrighi and Bordessoulle, while Marmont and Mortier would check his opponent's advance westward.

The two marshals, however, had already been forced to evacuate La Ferte-sous-Jouarre and had taken up their position round Meaux, leaving a strong rearguard at Trilport, while Bordessoulle had been driven back by the hostile cavalry. Blücher meanwhile had reached La Ferte-sous-Jouarre, and, constructing a couple of pontoon bridges a few miles below the town, had sent Kleist's corps across the Marne, to move round the bend of the river and threaten Mortier's left flank. On the 29th the bulk of Napoleon's force was between Sezanne and La Ferte Gaucher and he hoped to attack Blücher at La Ferte-sous-Jouarre on the following day, in conjunction with Marmont and Mortier.

The previous day, however, Kleist, moving round the bend of the Marne and advancing on Meaux from the north, had been defeated and driven back with the loss of over 1000 men by the two marshals, who had followed him some little distance up the Ourq. Blücher, who so far had only heard vague rumours that he was pursued by the Emperor in person, now crossed to the right bank of the Marne, destroyed the bridges and marched to support Kleist.

A variety of courses were open to him. He might (1) drive back the marshals and continue his advance through Meaux towards Paris; (2) march across their front to the Soissons-Paris road or retreat northward to effect his junction with Bulow and Winzingerode; (3) take up a defensive position and await attack.

Obviously his wisest course was to effect his junction with his reinforcement before offering battle, as his effective strength would be more than doubled, consequently he determined to fall back and sent orders to both Bulow and Winzingerode to advance to the Ourq, as he intended to offer battle in the neighbourhood of Ouchy. Thus it happened that when the French cavalry and horse artillery reached the Marne at La Ferte-sous-Jouarre on the afternoon of the 1st of March, they found the bridges broken down and saw only the hostile rearguard preparing to evacuate its position on the opposite bank of the river. Though Napoleon, with his main body, had covered just over seventy miles in four days, he had allowed Blücher too long a start and his project for driving him against the Marne had failed. The Emperor was still further delayed by the destruction of the bridges, and as he was without pontoons, this was a serious matter, while he was disagreeably surprised to learn that Schwarzenberg had again assumed the offensive and defeated Oudinot at Bar-sur-Aube. The marshals meanwhile had been reinforced by some 6000 men and 50 guns and had repulsed a fresh attack made by Kleist. Under the circumstances, Napoleon made up his mind to crush Blücher or drive him away to the northward and then march on Chalons, where he hoped to be able to

collect the garrisons from the fortresses in the Rhine
provinces, preparatory to acting vigorously against
Schwarzenberg's communications and thus bringing
his advance to a standstill.   Owing to the breaking
up of the frost, the roads were in a terrible state,
and as the army of Silesia had deliberately cut itself
adrift from its communications, the men were forced
to live on the country and pillaged the wretched
inhabitants unmercifully.

Meanwhile Bulow, advancing from Laon and Winzingerode, following the road from Reims through
Fismes, had agreed to make a combined attempt to
capture Soissons, but though Blücher was in communication with the Russian commander, he was
in considerable doubt as to Bulow's exact position.

Doubtful whether his reinforcements could arrive
in time, he now decided to join them on the right
bank of the Aisne, and sending on his baggage
through Fismes, ordered Winzingerode to select a
point for the construction of pontoon bridges, a little
above Soissons.   By the evening of the 3rd of March
the bridges at La Ferte-sous-Jouarre had been
repaired and the whole of the French force had
crossed the Marne.   Marmont, Mortier and Bordessoulle were approaching Ouchy from the west, while
Napoleon, with the bulk of his force, was a few miles
north of Chateau Thierry, having moved to his

right, as he was convinced that Blücher was endeavouring to reach Reims, and hoped to anticipate him in the neighbourhood of Fismes. Though Winzingerode's attempt to take Soissons by a *coup de main* had failed, the commandant, General Moreau, was so terrified by the threat of an immediate bombardment that he agreed to capitulate and evacuated the town on the afternoon of the 3rd of March. This was a piece of entirely unexpected good fortune for the Allies, as the garrison consisted of seasoned troops, the remnant of Poniatoski's Poles, some 1000 strong, while Marmont was so close at hand that his guns could be plainly heard, in action against the rearguard of the army of Silesia, as the garrison marched out of the town. Moreau had stipulated that he should be allowed to march out with the "honours of war," but one of the Russian officers remarked that under such circumstances it was customary to allow the garrison to take only two guns. Woronzoff, who overheard the remark, shrewdly observed that in the present case it would even be worth while to present Moreau with some of the Russian guns, provided he evacuated the town at once. Much has been said with regard to the French commandant's cowardice; in fact, it has generally been asserted that his shameful surrender saved the army of Silesia from disaster.

Undoubtedly the possession of the stone bridge over the Aisne at Soissons was of the utmost convenience to Blücher, but a careful comparison of the times and distances tends to prove that in any case the army of Silesia could have crossed the Aisne by means of the pontoon bridges without interference, except from the hostile cavalry. As a matter of fact, the Emperor had entirely failed to divine Blücher's intentions and had made a purposeless march eastward, under the impression that his opponent was endeavouring to reach Reims.

Even had Blücher been forced to fight before crossing the Aisne, his position, though extremely unfavourable, would have been by no means hopeless, for the opposing forces would have been of much the same strength and the iron veterans of the Silesian army would have proved themselves exceedingly formidable opponents. But it was typical of Napoleon to throw the whole blame for the miscarriage of his plans on his subordinates, though even if Moreau's conduct exercised little effect on the subsequent operations, nothing can palliate his gross dereliction of his obvious duty. Probably Marmont summed the situation up fairly accurately when he remarked that " it was an excellent opportunity to hang the commander of a fortress."

The army of Silesia completed its crossing,

practically unmolested, by the evening of the 4th of March, the war-scarred veterans, clothed in mud-stained rags, forming a marked contrast to the well-turned-out regiments belonging to Bulow's corps, which had hitherto seen little service.

The latter criticised Blücher's troops in the most unsparing fashion, writing that " The army is nearly starved, all discipline and order is dissolved and I confess to our shame that it looks not unlike a band of robbers."

The criticism was as unjust as it was ungenerous, for the army of Silesia had borne the brunt of Napoleon's vigorous blows and had been marching ceaselessly for the last two months, during exceptionally inclement weather.

Their uniforms doubtless were in tatters and their equipment worn out, but they had lost none of their soldierly qualities, and were ready to follow their leader to the end of the world, if necessary.

In his disgust at his opponent's escape, the Emperor issued a proclamation at Fismes, calling on the inhabitants of the neighbouring districts to take up arms and enjoining them to commence a guerrilla warfare against the invaders. Though he was aware that Blücher had at least 100,000 men concentrated on the heights north of Soissons, he nevertheless determined to attack him; consequently he left

Marmont to observe the latter town, sent a detachment under Corbineau to occupy Reims and, marching up the left bank of the Aisne with the bulk of his force, seized the crossing at Bery-au-Bac on the 5th of March. Though Blücher had succeeded in concentrating his whole available force, his position was still fraught with difficulty; he had temporarily abandoned his communications with the Rhine and was separated from Schwarzenberg by the occupation of Reims by a hostile detachment. His sole line of retreat ran through Laon; consequently the possession of the latter town had become of paramount importance to him. He fully intended to attack Napoleon at the first available opportunity, but was compelled to guard his right against a possible advance by Marmont, from the direction of Soissons.

He therefore ordered Bulow to take up a position covering Laon, while 6000 men from Langeron's corps were detailed as a garrison for Soissons, and Yorck, whose corps was to act as a general reserve, was stationed on the main road, some ten miles north of the latter town. The infantry of Winzingerode's corps, under Woronzoff, were drawn up on the heights west of Craone to check Napoleon's advance from Bery-au-Bac towards the Soissons-Laon road, while Winzingerode, with 10,000 mounted troops, was to move along the Laon-Bery-au-Bac road and envelop the French right. Blücher himself was with Sacken, whose corps was posted as a support some distance in rear of Woronzoff's position, while Kleist and Langeron, less the detachment left to garrison Soissons, were to follow Winzingerode and take part in the turning movement against the hostile right. Marmont meanwhile had attacked Soissons soon after daybreak on the 5th, and though his first attempt was repulsed, he had succeeded in fighting his way into the suburbs and commenced a vigorous assault on the fortifications. The Russians, however, offered a dogged resistance, and after a furious struggle, which lasted until dusk, forced their assailants to withdraw, with the loss of over 1500 men.

In spite of the failure of Marmont's attempt, Napoleon now determined to attack Woronzoff, though the latter's position was an extremely strong one and his troops had so far suffered neither loss nor fatigue.

After crossing the Aisne at Bery-au-Bac, the French army had wheeled to its left, so that it was about to fight facing Paris, while its opponents were drawn up with their backs towards their enemy's capital.

The village of Craone was situated at the eastern

extremity of a narrow plateau, which extended westward to the Soissons-Laon road ; to the north the ground fell sharply to the valley of the Lette, while to the south numerous small streams ran through precipitous ravines into the valley of the Aisne.

Craone itself was some five miles north-west of Bery-au-Bac, and along the whole length of the plateau ran the road known as the " Route des Dames," which eventually joined the main highway, half-way between Soissons and Laon.

The plateau varied considerably in width, occasionally becoming a mere ridge with a sharp drop on either side, into the valleys of the Lette and Aisne. Woronzoff had taken up his position about three miles from Craone, across the " Route des Dames " between Ailles and Vassogne, his main body, covered by the bulk of his artillery, being drawn up on the open ground immediately in rear of the narrowest part of the ridge. On his left, the village of Ailles itself, and the steep slopes above it, were held by a strong force of light troops, while on the opposite flank the spur jutting out towards Vassogne was occupied by a few squadrons and battalions, covered by a swarm of skirmishers.

Against a purely frontal attack, the position was almost impregnable, but the right flank was somewhat weak, as Woronzoff had not sufficient infantry to hold the long spur running southward past Vassogne with an adequate force. Blücher had intended to attack Napoleon on the morning of the 7th, and Winzingerode, followed by Kleist and Langeron, had commenced the turning movement, which was to decide the action, on the previous day, while the Prussian field-marshal had remained with a large body of mounted troops under Sacken, some distance in rear of Woronzoff's position.

Taking advantage of his numerical superiority, Napoleon determined to attack the hostile position simultaneously in front and on both flanks ; the main body was to advance along the plateau under his own command, while Ney, with three weak divisions, was to capture Ailles and then turn the hostile left. Nansouty, meanwhile, with a large force of mounted troops, was to gain the open ground on the spur above Vassogne and drive in the Russian right.

The battle commenced on the morning of the 7th with the advance of a formidable force of infantry along the " Route des Dames," covered by the fire of 100 guns, drawn up on the rising ground some little distance in rear of the farm of Heurtbize. The Russians, in their usual dense column formation, in three lines, suffered severely from the hostile artillery, but though the men were falling fast, they stood their ground with the utmost steadiness, while their guns played with deadly effect on the French infantry.

Led by Victor, the latter strove gallantly to close with their opponents, but they were unable to advance along the narrow ridge in face of rapid and accurate fire of the Russian artillery and eventually fell back with heavy loss.

Ney, meanwhile, pushing his attack with the greatest vigour, had driven his opponents from Ailles and his skirmishers gradually drove the Russian light troops up the steep slope above the village.

On the opposite flank, Nansouty had been forced to send his cavalry some considerable distance to his left to find a road on to the spur above Vassogne, while six battalions of infantry, who had endeavoured to scale the precipitous slope above the village, had been beaten back with heavy loss.

Blücher meanwhile had handed over the command to Sacken, and had started off to find Winzingerode, who ought to have already come into action against the French rear but who had only accomplished a short march on the previous day, on account of the heavy roads, and had then bivouacked a considerable distance from the field. As soon as Napoleon perceived that Ney's skirmishers had gained the crest of the plateau on the

Russian left, he ordered Victor to renew his attack along the " Route des Dames " and the French infantry pressed forward with such ardour that they captured one of the hostile batteries. Their success was only momentary, however, for Woronzoff launched a fierce counterstroke and a couple of Russian regiments, dashing forward with irresistible gallantry, recaptured the guns and drove back their opponents at the point of the bayonet.

Sacken, realising the formidable nature of the French attack, and seeing no signs of Winzingerode's expected diversion against the hostile rear, had already informed Blücher of the state of the battle and urgently requested reinforcements. He also ordered Woronzoff to retire, as the ammunition for the guns was running short, but the latter rightly judged that he ran less risk in holding his ground than in retiring across the open space in rear of his position, where Nansouty's cavalry could have acted with effect.

Shortly before two o'clock, however, Sacken heard from Blücher that a turning movement could not be completed in time and at once sent Woronzoff a direct order to retire. The latter general, sending back his wounded, then formed his infantry into squares and, in spite of the deadly fire of the French artillery, commenced his retreat in admirable order.

I

As soon as Napoleon saw the Russians preparing to move off, he hurried forward his guns and launched Nansouty's horsemen against the hostile squares.

The French troopers charged with such fury that it seemed that nothing could withstand their onslaught, but when the smoke cleared away, the hostile squares were still unshaken, while the few Russian squadrons charged gallantly to cover their comrades' retreat. Just before reaching the village of Cerny, Woronzoff selected an excellent position for his guns, where he drew them up in two tiers, sweeping the narrow ridge along which the road ran, and as the infantry reached the appointed spot, they halted and faced about, while the cavalry drew off to either flank. A deadly fire of grape, round shot and musketry instantly checked the French advance, and, after suffering appalling loss for over a quarter of an hour, they fell back in disorder.

Even the Guard, led by Ney and Victor, could not face the rapid and accurate fire of the hostile artillery, while Drouot, who had pushed his guns forward in close support of the infantry, was forced to limber up and retire out of range. As the wounded and useless guns were now well on their way toward Laon, Woronzoff drew off his heroic troops and retired unmolested, covered by Sacken's horsemen. So ended one of the most desperately contested battles in which Napoleon had ever taken part; the Russians were forced from their formidable position, but the victory was a barren one, for they left not a man nor a gun behind them and the French were much too shaken to pursue.

Sacken's infantry had taken no part in the battle, being, in fact, a considerable distance from the field, so that the numbers actually engaged were comparatively small but the casualties were enormous.

Out of 20,000 men actually under fire, the Russians lost 5000, while the French brought just over 30,000 men into the field, and lost 8000 ; such an appalling butcher's bill speaks volumes for the reckless courage with which both sides had fought.

Though the action was described in the bulletins as a decisive victory, Napoleon was in reality greatly chagrined by the useless slaughter, more especially as the casualties among the Guard had been unusually heavy, and it was impossible to replace the losses among his veteran troops.

Woronzoff had fought the action with remarkable skill and determination, while the steadiness and dogged courage of his heroic infantry had been beyond all praise. Blücher had been within an ace of inflicting a crushing defeat on his great opponent, for had not the turning movement miscarried, principally owing to Winzingerode's incapacity, coupled with faulty staff work, the French army would have found itself in a most critical situation. Blücher now determined to fall back and concentrate his entire force round Laon, the heights on which the town was situated offering an almost ideal position in which to accept battle.

The garrison of Soissons was withdrawn on the 8th of March, and the various corps of the Allied army moved into their allotted positions on the high ground round Laon, while the suburbs and neighbouring villages were occupied by a strong force of light troops.

Winzingerode was on the right, with his infantry drawn up in three lines and his cavalry posted on his outer flank and in rear of his centre; Bulow occupied the town and held the villages of Semilly and Ardon as advanced posts. Sacken and Langeron were in reserve, in rear of the centre, between Neuville and St Marcel, whilst Kleist and Yorck were on the left, the latter's outer flank being opposite the little town of Athies.

Altogether Blücher had about 110,000 men and 200 guns in position, while his line of battle was strengthened by the heights on which the town was situated and which formed a huge redoubt in his centre.

Including Marmont's detachment, Napoleon had

under 50,000 men, and his decision to attack double the number of veteran troops in a carefully selected position seems so hazardous that it could only have been justified by success. In reality his stroke at Blücher had failed, for the latter had succeeded in effecting his junction with his reinforcements and concentrating his entire force, so that the Emperor's action appears to have been due more to the desperation of a reckless gambler than to the well-considered boldness of a great commander. Nor were his dispositions such as might have been expected from the greatest master of modern warfare. The Emperor himself, advancing along the road from Soissons, was to attack the centre of the position; while Marmont, marching by the road from Reims, was to launch his attack from the direction of Athies, against the hostile left. The French army was thus divided into two isolated wings, the one under the Emperor's command being considerably the larger, and though the points selected for attack were some four miles apart, the gap was left entirely unoccupied.

On the 9th, Napoleon took up his position opposite the hostile centre, Ney being pushed well forward close to Semilly and Ardon, with the remainder of the infantry in support and the whole of the cavalry in reserve, immediately in rear. Under cover of a thick fog, Ney drove the hostile light troops from

Semilly and Ardon, but about eleven o'clock the sun burst through the mist and Blücher, realising the weakness of his opponent's force, determined to recapture the villages. Woronzoff attacked Semilly, while Bulow advanced against Ardon, and one of Winzingerode's divisions, supported by the whole of his cavalry, fell on the French left.

Overwhelmed by numbers, Ney's men were driven back in confusion for a considerable distance, and the pursuit was only checked by a vigorous charge, delivered by the Guard and the reserve cavalry, which forced the Allies to retire to their original position. When, about four o'clock, Napoleon was informed that Marmont was approaching Athies, he immediately brought forward the Guard, and after a sharp skirmish drove the hostile light troops from Clarcy and Ardon, while he also gained possession of the Abbey of St Vincent, on the heights overlooking the latter village.

Marmont meanwhile had arrived on the field from Bery-au-Bac and after a desperate struggle driven one of Yorck's divisions from Athies, though not before a large number of the houses had been set on fire.

Except for the local counterstroke, which had recaptured the villages in front of his centre, Blücher had remained on the defensive, as he was somewhat mystified by his opponent's dispositions, and it was late in the afternoon before he could persuade himself that Napoleon had no troops in the centre to connect his isolated wings.

Darkness put an end to the battle, and the French remained in possession of Clarcy and Ardon, though they had been unable to capture Semilly, while Marmont allowed his men, exhausted by their twelve hours' marching and fighting, to bivouac round Athies, without taking any precautions against surprise.

Blücher determined to crush the isolated French right and ordered Langeron and Sacken to move to their left and take up their position between Laon and Chambry to support the attack, which was to be carried out by the whole of the left wing, under the direction of Yorck.

The latter general had also realised the opportunity presented by Marmont's unsupported corps and had sent a messenger to Blücher to obtain his sanction for the proposed movement. Thus as soon as he received his orders, he formed the whole of his infantry into a mass of columns at close intervals, with Kleist's corps in close support, while the cavalry and horse artillery were posted well forward on his left, so as to be in a position to take up the pursuit at once. Covered by the darkness, the

Prussians quietly moved into their positions, totally unobserved by their opponents, and Yorck issued a written order : " Not a shot shall be fired ; the attack is to be made with bayonets alone." Advancing in perfect order and complete silence, the Prussians suddenly fell on their unsuspecting opponents with a loud hurrah and Marmont's wretched conscripts, who were sleeping heavily after their exertions, were scattered and driven from the field in hopeless confusion.

Zieten's troopers at once took up the pursuit, capturing nearly 3000 dazed fugitives, who were much too astonished by the sudden onslaught to think of attempting the least resistance.

The night attack had been planned and carried out by Yorck in the most brilliant manner, and the French force had been so completely overthrown that Marmont reported to Napoleon at 2 A.M. : " We have not been able to restore order to the different bodies of troops, which are all mingled together and in no condition to carry out any evolution or perform any service." [1]

Blücher was delighted at Yorck's success, and wrote : " Your Excellency has once more shown what clearness of mind combined with decision can

[1] " Blücher," pp. 239-240 (Heroes of the Nations Series, E. F. Henderson).

accomplish."[1] He also ordered Yorck and Kleist to take up the pursuit at once and strike at Marmont's right flank, but these were the last orders that the veteran Prussian marshal was destined to issue for some time.

The strain of the last two months had been enormous, while the difficulties and dangers had been aggravated by the fact that the political situation was most involved and that it was impossible to rely either on Schwarzenberg's co-operation or support. Suffering severely from ague, coupled with a violent inflammation of the eyes, he had been totally unlike his own vigorous self during the day's fighting, and, oppressed by the dread of the sudden appearance of a strong hostile force from some unknown direction, his tactics had been marked by an unusual hesitation and he had omitted to seize the opportunity of overwhelming Napoleon's comparatively weak force.

During the night Blücher completely collapsed, but his illness was kept a secret as long as possible by Gneisenau, who found himself in a most difficult position, for he was junior to both Langeron and Yorck.

The former, besides being absolutely incompetent, was merely the commander of the Russian detachment serving with the army of Silesia, while

[1] " Blücher," pp. 239-240 (Heroes of the Nations Series, E. F. Henderson).

the latter, though a most capable general, was so quarrelsome and self-willed that Gneisenau could never have worked in harmony with him.

In the desperate situation in which Napoleon found himself, the average leader would have thought of nothing but escape and would probably have retreated in haste during the early hours of the 10th, but Napoleon chose the bolder and in reality the safer course. He argued that an immediate retreat would certainly be the signal for thousands of his conscripts to desert, and would infallibly bring the whole of the army of Silesia on his heels, while a vigorous attack, though it could not possibly lead to a decisive success, might at least impose on his opponents for some time, and would, in any case, take the pressure from Marmont's shaken troops.

Blücher had ordered Bulow and Winzingerode to advance against Napoleon on the morning of the 10th, and Chernicheff, with the latter's advance guard, had even driven a French division from Clarcy, but Gneisenau was so impressed by the boldness with which the French force was handled that he not only countermanded the proposed attack but also recalled Yorck from his pursuit of Marmont. Finding himself unsupported, Chernicheff was compelled to fall back to the foot of the heights, and Napoleon commenced a vigorous attack on the centre of the hostile position. The French infantry pressed forward with the greatest gallantry but were eventually brought to a standstill by the deadly fire of the formidable array of artillery posted on the heights and of the infantry holding the villages at the foot of the slope.

Early in the afternoon the Emperor had ordered the baggage and reserve artillery to retreat to Soissons, and about four o'clock the French troops, after suffering heavily, commenced to retire. Owing to the confusion caused by Blücher's complete breakdown, the Allies made no attempt to pursue their opponents, and Napoleon fell back towards Soissons unmolested.

His carefully planned and vigorously carried out attack on Blücher had ended in hopeless failure. He had lost some 16,000 men since crossing the Aisne on the 5th, and only been saved from an overwhelming disaster by the sudden prostration of his doughty antagonist.

Absolute confusion reigned at the headquarters of the army of Silesia. Blücher was supposed to have lost his reason or to be on the point of death, and even the loyal Sacken was of opinion that "the field-marshal had completely lost his head." At this critical moment Yorck, who was always prone to consider himself slighted, and who had been brooding over his annoyance at not being allowed to follow up his success against Marmont, announced his intention of withdrawing from the army. He had actually entered his coach, and was preparing to set out for Brussels, when he received an almost illegible note from Blücher, who with the greatest difficulty had managed to write the few words : " Old comrade, history should not relate such things of us. Be sensible and come back." [1] Yorck was deeply touched and at once abandoned his journey, writing the following thoroughly characteristic epistle to his chief:—"Your Excellency's personal letter is the expression of your upright heart, which I always did and always will esteem. This very uprightness, indeed, must tell you how painful it is to a man who feels his worth and is conscious of no wrong to have received a slight. I have returned to my post. I will continue to fight as long as there is need but then will gladly give way to the arrogant and the theorists. From the bottom of my heart and with sincere sympathy I wish you a speedy restoration to health." [2]

Blücher had meanwhile fallen into a hopeless state of weakness and lethargy. He took no interest in the operations and was incapable of issuing any orders,

[1] " Blücher " (Heroes of the Nations Series, E. F. Henderson).
[2] *Ibid.*

so that the command of his army practically devolved on his capable chief of the staff.

Gneisenau's task was no easy one. The army had lost its leader and the men were exhausted by want of food and the continual marching over roads ankle-deep in mud, while neither Langeron nor Yorck afforded him the slightest assistance; indeed, the latter cavilled at every order he issued.

Under the circumstances, he wisely determined to give the army a little much-needed rest and an opportunity of collecting supplies, while he considered, with a good deal of justice, that it was time the Grand Army took a more vigorous share in the operations, for so far the army of Silesia had borne the whole brunt of the campaign.

Though the failure of his stroke at Blücher had in reality rendered his cause hopeless, Napoleon never for a moment lost his courage, and within three days he struck fiercely and successfully at his opponents, in a quite unexpected direction. The Emperor remained at Soissons for two days to reorganise his shaken troops, while he determined on his future course of action, but during the evening of the 12th, he learned that an opportunity had arisen for falling upon an isolated corps, moving to support the army of Silesia.

St Priest, with some 13,000 Russian troops, had

marched from the Rhine to Chalons, where he had been ordered to remain to keep open the communications between Blücher and Schwarzenberg. When Napoleon had concentrated his whole force for his attack on Laon, the Russian general had determined to recapture Reims, which had been left with only a weak garrison.

The French commander was unable to defend the town with under 2000 partially trained conscripts, and was forced to surrender after a slight resistance. St Priest's success was extremely valuable, as it opened up a shorter line of communications between the Allied armies and seriously deranged Napoleon's designs.

The Emperor determined to recapture the town. He then intended to withdraw the garrisons from the fronter fortresses and with these troops and the Guard to threaten Schwarzenberg's communications with the Rhine, while Mortier, with some 30,000 men, largely composed of conscripts, contained Blücher.

After his disaster at Athies, Marmont had retreated to Fismes, and on the morning of the 13th, the Emperor marched from Soissons to join him, with the intention of surprising the Russian force holding Reims.

St Priest, who had heard of the result of the

fighting round Laon, and imagined that Napoleon had retreated towards Paris, never for an instant expected an attack, and had consequently allowed his men to billet themselves in the villages outside the city. On the afternoon of the 13th, his outposts reported the approach of a hostile force, but the Russian commander imagined that they could only be stragglers from Marmont's detachment and took no immediate precautions against attack.

However, Marmont, who was with the advance guard of the French force, drove in the Russian outpost during the afternoon, and St Priest hurriedly formed up his men in front of the town. Napoleon, with the main body, had not yet arrived on the field, and Marmont completely deceived his opponent by feigning to withdraw his advanced troops. St Priest was now convinced that he had only a small force to deal with, and in spite of the assurance of one of the prisoners that Napoleon was at hand with his whole force, he turned to his staff and exclaimed boastfully : " He will not step over 14,000 men. You need not ask which way to retire—there will be no retreat." [1]

He was, however, speedily to be undeceived, for the Emperor had now arrived, and the whole French force advanced to the attack ; a formidable mass of

[1] Alison, " History of Europe," vol. ii., p. 265.

horsemen was hurled against the Russian left, while Marmont, supported by the Guard, advanced along the main road from Fismes.

St Priest had drawn up his men in two lines outside the suburbs, but was soon compelled to retire in face of greatly superior force arrayed against him, and was mortally wounded while directing the retreat.

This caused considerable confusion, of which the French cavalry took the fullest advantage, and a disaster seemed inevitable.

The Riazan Regiment, however, formed square and covered the retreat of their comrades with the most heroic gallantry, and eventually cut their way through their opponents, bearing with them their dying general.

General Emmanuel promptly rallied the fugitives and prepared to defend the town, while his men seconded his efforts so gallantly that they kept their opponents at bay for a considerable time.

Learning that he was almost surrounded, General Emmanuel decided to evacuate the town, and drew off his men shortly before midnight, part of the force retiring to Chalons, while a portion managed to elude their opponents and eventually joined Blücher at Laon.

Napoleon entered the city at one A.M. on the

morning of the 14th, amid the enthusiastic cheers of his troops and of the inhabitants.

His success had been singularly complete, for he had recaptured the city at the cost of little over 800 men, while, including prisoners, the Allies had lost over 3500 men altogether, with 11 guns and a quantity of ammunition. That the Emperor should have been able to achieve such surprising results with troops discouraged by the heavy losses and want of success in the recent fighting at Craone and round Laon is surely one of the greatest triumphs of his remarkable career, and speaks volumes for his powers as a leader of men.

He remained at Reims for a couple of days, while Ney followed the remnant of Russian corps as far as Chalons. The Emperor had once again succeeded in interposing between Schwarzenberg and Blücher, and with the Rhine provinces, which had hitherto escaped the ravages of war, to draw on, was in an excellent position for carrying out his scheme of forcing Schwarzenberg to retreat by harrying his communications. Reims was the last city which the Emperor was destined to capture, but this final flicker of success was of considerable value, as it seriously alarmed the Austrian commander and to a great extent atoned for the failure of the operations against Blücher.

K

CHAPTER VII

NAPOLEON'S SECOND ATTACK ON SCHWARZENBERG

Schwarzenberg sends a Detachment to secure his Communications and crush Augereau—The Grand Army again advances on Paris—Macdonald is forced to abandon the Line of the Seine—Napoleon marches against Schwarzenberg—The Grand Army retreats and concentrates round Troyes — Schwarzenberg determines to assume the Offensive—The Battle of Arcis-sur-Aube—Napoleon retreats to Vitry and threatens Schwarzenberg's Communications—The Allies march on Vitry—Blücher marches to Chalons—The Czar determines to advance on Paris

WHILE Napoleon and Blücher were engaged in a deadly struggle on the Aisne, Schwarzenberg's strategy had been marked by its habitual lethargy and timidity. His first care was to secure his communications with the Rhine, for which purpose he had ordered the formation of a fresh force, termed " the Army of the South," which consisted of some 50,000 men under the Prince of Hesse-Homburg and was composed of the Austrian and German reserves as well as the 1st Corps, commanded by Bianchi. He then concentrated the remainder of his force in the vicinity of Chaumont, prepared to retreat at once to Langres, should it appear

146

probable that Napoleon intended to advance against him.

When he learned that the Emperor had left Troyes and marched northward with a large proportion of his force in pursuit of the army of Silesia, he decided to adopt a cautious offensive against the hostile troops in the valley of the Seine.

He had been influenced in his decision by the King of Prussia, who was naturally most anxious that Napoleon should be prevented from massing his whole force against Blücher in the valley of the Marne and had ceaselessly urged Schwarzenberg to make an effective diversion by a vigorous advance south of the Seine. On the morning of the 27th of February the corps of Wittgenstein and Wrede, together about 35,000 strong, advanced along the road from Chaumont towards Bar-sur-Aube. Oudinot, who could muster only some 17,000 men, had taken up an unsuitable position on the eastern bank of the river, with his right resting on the town itself. Wittgenstein intended to make a frontal attack with Gortschakoff's division, while Eugene of Wurtemberg, supported by a formidable body of mounted troops under Count Pahlen, turned the French left and threatened their communications.

Oudinot, however, had no intention of adopting a purely passive defensive, and seized the heights

of Ailleville, thus interposing between the two portions of the hostile force. Wittgenstein promptly
ordered the position to be stormed, and after a fierce
struggle the Russian infantry drove their opponents
from the heights and the attack developed along the
whole of the French front. Seeing that Gorts-
schakoff's infantry had been left without support,
Oudinot ordered forward Kellermann's veteran
cuirassiers, who had recently arrived from the
Spanish frontier, and the French troopers charged
so fiercely that they threw the hostile infantry into
hopeless confusion.

The whole centre began to waver and Wittgenstein
was obliged to concentrate the fire of his entire
artillery to check the French counterstroke, while he
sent an urgent message to Pahlen to return at once.

The deadly fire of the Russian batteries drove
back Kellermann's cuirassiers with heavy loss,
while Schwarzenberg, arriving on the field in person,
ordered two brigades of cavalry and a brigade of
infantry from Wrede's corps to support the centre.
Pahlen was ordered to countermarch and to turn
the hostile left, while Wrede, coming into action
against the opposite flank, commenced a vigorous
attack on the town of Bar.

Hopelessly outnumbered, and menaced on both
flanks, Oudinot was forced to retire, but his troops

offered a most dogged resistance, especially in Bar itself, where some sanguinary street fighting took place.

He handled his men with ability, and under cover of darkness retreated across the Aube unmolested, for Pahlen's powerful force of mounted troops had spent the day marching uselessly backward and forward between the centre and extreme right of the Allied line.

The losses on either side amounted to about 2500, though the French left a considerable number of prisoners in their opponents' hands, but on the whole they may be considered to have been fortunate to have escaped an overwhelming disaster. Nevertheless the victory was very welcome, for it entirely restored the confidence of the rank and file of the Grand Army, whose *moral* had been seriously shaken by continual retreat in face of a vastly inferior force.

Schwarzenberg had acted with considerable determination and had received a slight wound during the latter part of the engagement, while Wittgenstein had been so severely wounded that he was unable to take any further part in the campaign and was succeded in command of the Russian corps by General Raeffskoi. Though he received his well-earned marshal's baton from the Czar in recognition of his share in the victory, it was most unfortunate that he was unable to take part in the triumphal entry into the French capital a month later. By no means a great general, for he was prone to undue rashness and too impatient to carefully work out his plans, Wittgenstein was nevertheless a very capable and energetic commander, without a particle of jealousy in his composition, and his enforced retirement was a very real loss to the Grand Army. After his brief outbursts of energy, Schwarzenberg promptly relapsed into his habitual torpor and allowed Oudinot to fall back to Troyes unmolested, on the ground that it was unsafe to continue the advance until Macdonald's intentions had been ascertained. As a matter of fact, the force under the latter marshal, in the neighbourhood of Vandœuvres, was so weak that it was eventually defeated by the mounted troops under Pahlen and driven towards Troyes. It was now definitely reported that Napoleon had quitted the valley of the Seine with a large body of troops and that only a comparatively small force had been left in the neighbourhood of Troyes.

Meanwhile the congress at Chatillon had been wearily dragging out its useless existence, for the Emperor had never intended to make peace except on his own terms and was only making use of Caulaincourt's abilities to gain time.

His successes during February had made him increasingly arrogant, and even Metternich was at last convinced that he would never consent to any settlement which would establish a balance of power in Europe, with Austria in a predominant position. A meeting of the plenipotentiaries of the various powers was held at Chaumont and a treaty drawn up by which Great Britain, Russia, Prussia and Austria mutually agreed to each keep 150,000 men in the field during the continuation of the campaign and that none of the powers should conclude a separate peace.

This put an end to the useless proceedings at Chatillon, and the treaty was in reality the turning-point of the campaign, for it entirely obviated the danger of Austria making a separate peace with Napoleon and abandoning her Allies.

On the 1st of March, Schwarzenberg issued orders for a general advance, and the headquarters of the Grand Army were moved to Bar-sur-Aube, while preparations were made for an attack on Troyes.

Macdonald had meanwhile joined Oudinot and assumed command of the whole force, which amounted to some 35,000 men, of whom more than a quarter were excellent cavalry. He took up a carefully selected position covering the city, on an elevated plateau, the approach to which was usually rendered difficult by marshes on the front and flank, though in the present instance this advantage was neutralised by the severe frost, which rendered the marshes easily passable by all arms. Schwarzenberg issued orders for the attack to take place on the morning of the 3rd of March; Wrede was to advance along the main road from Vandœuvres against the front of the position, while Wittgenstein's corps and Eugene of Wurtemberg made a wide turning movement against the hostile left and rear.

As usual, Schwarzenberg procrastinated, and though the 60,000 men with whom he meant to carry out the attack were in position early in the forenoon, he did not give the actual order to advance until three o'clock.

Hardly had the action commenced when the French left, seeing itself in danger of being turned by Wurtemberg's rapid advance, began to retreat towards the town. Pahlen's cuirassiers dashed forward, riding over a couple of battalions and pushing their advance up to the outskirts of Troyes, where they captured a number of guns. St Germain now charged fiercely with his dragoons, driving back the Russian horsemen and recapturing several of the guns, but the advance of large bodies of the Allied infantry forced the French left to retire. The centre now commenced to fall back, and as soon as Schwarzenberg perceived their intention, he ordered Wrede to storm the bridge over the Barse and the latter general, leading his Bavarians with great dash, drove his opponents from the heights.

Finding that he could hold his position no longer, Macdonald agreed to evacuate Troyes on the following day, and was permitted to withdraw unmolested. His losses amounted to about 2000 men, of whom, however, quite two-thirds were prisoners, and a few guns, while the Allies' casualties were under 800.

The headquarters of the Grand Army were moved to Troyes on the 5th of March, while Macdonald fell back along the valley of the Seine, holding the bridges at Nogent, Bray and Montereau, with small detachments, and establishing his headquarters at Provins.

Schwarzenberg was now within six marches of Paris, and his 80,000 men were in the highest spirits after their easy successes at Bar and Troyes, but though there were only some 30,000 defeated and dispirited French troops to oppose his advance, the Austrian leader could not make up his mind to assume a vigorous offensive. Though the military situation urgently demanded a determined advance, he once again had recourse to his favourite manœuvre, a wide turning movement, and ordered Wrede, Wurtemberg and Wittgenstein's corps, under Raeff-skoi, to advance to the line of the Yonne, between Sens and Pont-sur-Yonne. The Czar, who thoroughly realised that the struggle between Napoleon and Blücher, in the valley of the Marne, would decide the issue of the campaign, strongly disapproved of the movement to the south, and wished the Grand Army to incline to its right, so as to be in a position to support the Prussian marshal.

On the 8th of March he wrote to Schwarzenberg, setting forth his views as follows :—" The Emperor considers that the advance of the Grand Army to Sens is drawing us away from the enemy, and that it is therefore indispensable to direct all our forces to the right towards Arcis, between that town and Vitry : and, at all events, to reinforce them with the reserves, which should be ordered to move forward." [1]

On the 11th, he wrote in even stronger terms : " In consequence of intelligence received from Field-Marshal Blücher, the Emperor considers it indispensable to begin to move by the right, between Vitry and Arcis-sur-Aube." [2]

[1] Alison, " History of Europe," vol. xi., p. 250.
[2] *Ibid.*

Schwarzenberg, however, could be extremely obstinate and absolutely refused to abandon his leisurely advance south of the Seine to take part in the stirring events farther to the north.

Yet another attempt was made to persuade him to act with energy, Prince Volkonsky, the Czar's aide-de-camp, writing on the 14th: " I hasten to communicate to your Highness the reports received from Count St Priest. His Majesty has charged me to inform you that, according to his opinion, it is now more necessary than ever to act on the offensive. Henceforth your hands will be completely unbound, and you may act according to military calculation." [1]

Schwarzenberg's unfortunate inability to adopt any decided course of action is clearly shown by one of his letters, written at this period: " I have no news and I confess that I tremble. If Blücher suffers a defeat how can I myself give battle ? For if I am conquered what a triumph for Napoleon ! And what a humiliation for the sovereigns to recross the Rhine at the head of a beaten army." [2] However, even the leisurely advance of the Allies in the valley of the Seine at last began to produce some effect and Macdonald wrote to the Minister of War,

[1] " Blücher " (Heroes of the Nations Series, E. F. Henderson).
[2] *Ibid.*

at Paris : " My left is outflanked and I am forced to evacuate Provins in order to cover Nangis. I shall defend the ground every inch of the way, but am in urgent need of reinforcements." [1]

Schwarzenberg, however, was not entirely responsible for the tardy advance of the Grand Army, for news of Napoleon's failure to crush Blücher had reached the Allied headquarters and diplomacy once more made its baneful influence felt. Metternich hoped that Napoleon's want of success on the Aisne might have brought him to a reasonable frame of mind and that he might now be willing to conclude peace, on condition that France was confined to her original frontiers.

Napoleon, meanwhile, had remained at Reims until the 16th of March, and had received a most welcome reinforcement of 6000 men, drawn from the garrisons of the fortresses in the Ardennes. Great efforts were made to induce the peasantry to undertake guerrilla warfare against the Allies, though with comparatively little success, while Ney, from Chalons, sent officers to the commanders of fortresses on the Rhine, instructing them to cut their way through the blockading forces and bring their garrisons to join the field army.

The army of Silesia had remained round Laon

---

[1] " Blücher " (Heroes of the Nations Series, E. F. Henderson).

since the action on the 11th, as Blücher was still too ill to issue orders and Gneisenau was determined that the men should enjoy a little much-needed rest and have an opportunity of collecting supplies.

Napoleon was faced by a most difficult situation, for though his success at Reims had in a measure atoned for the failure of his operations against Blücher, and he had once more interposed between the two hostile armies, yet the army of Silesia, at Laon, was as near Paris as he was himself, while the Grand Army in the valley of the Seine was considerably nearer.

It would obviously be most dangerous to attack Blücher again or even to make a flank march across his front to interpose between the Grand Army and Paris. The latter, however, had to be checked immediately, as it was obvious that Macdonald's weak force was quite insufficient to prevent their occupying the French capital, and this would be the signal for the utter collapse of Napoleon's regime. The Emperor decided to return to the valley of the Seine, being well aware that a serious threat at Schwarzenberg's communications was the surest way of forcing him to beat a precipitate retreat and the most effective means of safeguarding the French capital.

It was necessary, however, to prevent Blücher

making a sudden dash at Paris with his cavalry and light troops while he himself marched against the rear of the Grand Army, and for this purpose a force some 20,000 strong, under Marmont and Mortier, was left on the Aisne, with instructions to retard the advance of the army of Silesia as long as possible.

The Emperor marched to Epernay with about 25,000 men on the 17th and reached Fere-Champenoise by the next evening, while, confident that his advance would cause his opponent to concentrate his force and retreat, he ordered Macdonald and Oudinot to join him.

For the second time within a month, Schwarzenberg was completely surprised and caught with his army widely distributed, for he had extended his force on both banks of the Seine, from Sens almost as far as Sezanne.

The news of Napoleon's advance threw the Allied headquarters into a state of hopeless panic, but fortunately the Czar hastened from Troyes to Arcis, where he found Schwarzenberg confined to his bed by a severe attack of gout, and orders were instantly issued for a general concentration north of Troyes, while Wrede was instructed to hold the bridge over the Aube at Arcis at all costs.

Fortunately for the Allies, Napoleon bore off to his right to capture Plancy, where he had ordered

Macdonald and Oudinot to join him, for had he forced the passage of the Aube at Arcis on the 19th, he would have caught the Grand Army in the act of concentration and almost certainly have scored a decisive success. Schwarzenberg, however, rising to the occasion, adopted a bold and vigorous line of action ; he countermanded the instructions already issued for retreat and ordered a concentration of his whole force between Plancy and Arcis.

Napoleon, who was entirely unprepared for such vigorous action on the part of his opponents, determined to march up both banks of the Aube to Arcis, or, if necessary, to Bar, and to sever effectively his adversaries' communications through Chaumont and Langres.

He arrived opposite to Arcis on the morning of the 20th and at once occupied the town, for Wrede had now been ordered to fall back for a short distance towards Troyes and avoid becoming engaged until he could be effectively supported. Contrary to his usual custom, the Emperor held a council of war, and though the inhabitants were unanimous in stating that the Allies had abandoned all idea of retreat and would shortly appear before the town in considerable force, he could not bring himself to believe that Schwarzenberg would adopt such a determined course of action.

He was confirmed in this view by the fact that Wrede had abandoned the town, and consequently ordered his mounted troops to cross to the southern bank of the Aube and pursue what he imagined to be a weak rearguard, along the road to Troyes.

In reality Schwarzenberg's bold decision had entirely changed the situation, and Wrede's corps now formed the right wing of the Grand Army, which was concentrated a short distance south of the Aube, between Plancy and Arcis.

The Czar, accompanied by the King of Prussia, had, meanwhile, arrived on the high ground near Menil-la-Comtesse, some few miles south of Arcis, where his Guards had already taken up their position. The events of the last few days had caused him an enormous amount of anxiety, and as he was walking with Barclay de Tolly, he pointed to some of the Austrian generals and exclaimed : " These gentlemen have made my head half grey. Napoleon will amuse us here with insignificant movements, and meanwhile march the main body of his forces on Brienne and fall on our communications." [1]

The battle commenced with a skirmish between the French cavalry under Sebastiani and some Russian squadrons, but both sides brought up reinforcements and several batteries of horse artillery.

[1] Alison, " History of Europe," vol. xi., p. 325.

For some time neither side gained any material advantage, but eventually the French horsemen, overpowered by weight of numbers, were driven in confusion towards the Aube.

Realising the gravity of the situation, Napoleon crossed the river and, taking up his position, sword in hand, at the entrance to the town, exclaimed : " Let me see which of you will pass me." His fearless bearing checked the retreat, which was rapidly degenerating into a panic-stricken flight, while Friant, bringing his division across the bridge and through the streets of Arcis at the double, deployed in front of the town and the steady fire of his men forced the Allied horsemen to beat a hasty retreat.

Napoleon now brought the remainder of his force across the Aube and took up his position, astride the road from Troyes, on the heights south of the town, with his flanks thrown back towards the river at Villette and Torchy respectively.

He had no intention of fighting a pitched battle, as he had not yet been joined by Macdonald, whose troops were scattered along the right bank of the Seine, guarding the bridges from Montereau to Pont-sur-Seine, but was still under the delusion that he was only engaged with a strong rearguard, covering the retreat of the Grand Army towards Bar-sur-Aube.

A fierce struggle now commenced between Ney

L

and Wrede for the possession of Torchy ; an Austrian
battalion carried the village, but were promptly
driven out, whereupon Wrede, bringing up three
fresh battalions, succeeded in capturing the position
after a series of furious assaults.   Ney was falling
back towards Arcis, when he was reinforced by
several battalions of the Guard ; promptly turning
about, he made a furious attack on the village,
once more ejected the hostile infantry and maintained his position during the night, in spite of a
violent bombardment and a vigorous attack delivered by a couple of battalions of the Russian
guard.

During the day some 2000 of Macdonald's cavalry
had arrived and the Emperor now placed them under
Sebastiani's orders and sent the whole of his mounted
troops against the hostile centre on the road to
Troyes.

In spite of the darkness, Sebastiani charged the
Russian cavalry with the greatest fury, driving them
from the field and throwing some Bavarian squadrons
into confusion.   He then wheeled to his left, overthrew some Austrian cavalry and was about to
attack Wrede's infantry, but was brought to a standstill by the steady volleys of a battalion of Russian
grenadiers and the accurate fire of several batteries.   The Allied cavalry meanwhile had rallied and

Sebastiani's gallant squadrons were attacked by an
overwhelming mass of Russian, Prussian and Austrian
horsemen but managed to fight their way back with
comparatively little loss and bivouacked behind the
extreme right of their own infantry. The Allies had
brought a formidable force of artillery into action
late in the afternoon, and after silencing the French
guns, a destructive fire was opened on the infantry
holding the outskirts of Arcis, part of the town as
well as the village of Torchy being set on fire by the
vigorous bombardment. Shortly after 10 P.M. the
firing ceased altogether, and both armies bivouacked
on the field of battle; so far the Allies, in spite of
their great numerical superiority, had gained little
advantage, as only Wrede's corps, the cavalry,
artillery and part of the Russian Guard had been
seriously engaged. The left wing, consisting of the
3rd, 4th and 6th Corps, under the Prince of Wurtemberg, had taken no part in battle, as, owing to misunderstanding, its leader had directed his march
towards Plancy and become engaged in a desultory
skirmish with a portion of Macdonald's force and
eventually bivouacked some seven miles west of
Arcis. Still obstinately adhering to his opinion
that he was only opposed by a strong rearguard,
Napoleon held his position south of the Aube during
the night of the 20th-21st of March and sent

orders to Macdonald to join him as soon as possible. Schwarzenberg's orders, issued shortly before midnight, should have brought Wurtemberg's three corps into position on Wrede's left soon after daybreak on the 21st, but they were delayed in transmission and Wurtemberg's march was hampered by the action of the French cavalry against his left flank, so that he did not reach his allotted position before ten o'clock. The Allied army was hidden by the conformation of the ground, consequently Napoleon was confirmed in the erroneous idea and ordered Sebastiani to advance, supported by Ney. As soon as the former reached the summit of the plateau, he beheld the Allies, some 75,000 strong, drawn up in readiness to advance on either side of the road from Troyes to Arcis.

Napoleon at last realised the danger of his position, recalled Ney and at once determined to transfer his troops to the right bank of the Aube ; a bridge of boats was hastily constructed at Villette and shortly before two o'clock the Guard commenced to cross. They were to be followed by a strong force of cavalry, while another division of infantry and the reserve artillery used the wooden bridge at Arcis. Macdonald was ordered to take up a position near Plancy and cover the crossings in the neighbourhood, while Oudinot was to remain on the right bank of the

Aube to prevent the Allies forcing a passage at Arcis.

Though Schwarzenberg had his men in position before eleven o'clock, he was unable to make up his mind to give the signal to advance until three o'clock, when it was clear that the hostile force had commenced to retreat to the opposite bank of the river. The whole of the formidable artillery was pushed forward, and opened a most destructive fire, while Pahlen drove Sebastiani across the Aube at Villette with heavy loss, but the former succeeded in destroying the bridge and so checked the pursuit.

Meanwhile Leval's men held Arcis with the most determined gallantry, and in spite of their enormous superiority in numbers, it was late in the evening before the Allies succeeded in forcing their way into the town.

Even then the French infantry offered a desperate resistance, and after some sanguinary street fighting, a large number managed to effect their retreat to the opposite bank of the river and burn the bridge behind them.

During the night the French artillery on the northern bank of the Aube kept up such a hot fire that the Allies were unable to repair the bridge, while Wrede, who had been ordered to ford the river above the town, was only able to get his cavalry across, his infantry being obliged to march up the left bank until they reached the bridge at Lesmont. Covered by Oudinot, opposite Arcis, and Macdonald on his right, the main body of the French army fell back unmolested towards Sompuis, on their way to Vitry.

Schwarzenberg completely lost touch with the main body of the hostile force, having not the least idea whether Napoleon had retreated towards Vitry or Chalons or had doubled back to Sezanne, to interpose between the Allies and Paris. Though he had shown considerable decision in concentrating his whole available force to attack Napoleon, he had displayed all his wonted hesitation on the actual field of battle, but his task had been a somewhat difficult one, for the Czar had on this occasion been strongly opposed to offering battle, as he imagined that Napoleon would merely leave a rearguard at Arcis and move down the right bank of the Aube towards Bar with his main body. Undoubtedly Schwarzenberg missed an excellent opportunity of inflicting a crushing reverse on his redoubtable antagonist, and had allowed the latter to extricate himself from a most critical situation with comparatively little loss. Throughout the whole of the following day the French rearguard remained in position opposite Arcis, and Wurtemberg, abandoning the idea of forcing a passage, left Gyulai to observe them and crossed the Aube a few miles higher up with the 4th and 6th Corps.

Meanwhile Napoleon, who had determined to revert to his original plan of collecting the garrisons from the fortresses in the Rhine provinces and then falling on Schwarzenberg's communications, had marched through Sompuis to Vitry, intending to move down the right bank of the Marne to Chaumont and place himself astride his opponents' line of retreat through Langres to the Upper Rhine. He received an unexpected check, however, at Vitry, for the garrison, some 5000 strong, refused to surrender to Ney, and after a futile bombardment the marshal was ordered to observe the fortress and send his mounted troops across the Marne to St Dizier.

At dusk on the 22nd, Napoleon was between Vitry and St Dizier, Ney a little south of the former town and Macdonald still in position north of Arcis.

The 4th, 5th and 6th Corps of the Grand Army were round Brebant, on the road to Vitry, with the Guard and reserves some distance to their right rear. Gyulai was at Arcis with a strong force of mounted troops on his left, towards Plancy.

During the night of the 22nd–23rd, Macdonald evacuated his position unobserved and moved northwards towards Sommesous, being forced to make a considerable detour, as a large force of hostile cavalry blocked his direct road to Vitry.

Though most of his artillery and ammunition park, which had been sent on in advance, fell into the hands of the Russian horsemen, the marshal himself, in spite of being continually harassed during his march, managed to cross the Marne a little above Vitry. By the evening of the 23rd, Napoleon had reached St Dizier with the Guard, while Ney, followed by Macdonald, was on the march from Vitry and the bulk of the cavalry were spread out along the right bank of the Marne in the direction of Chaumont.

The main body of the Allies, advancing on Vitry from the west and south, halted some little distance in front of Sompuis, thus effectually interposing between Napoleon and the detachments under Marmont, Mortier and Pacthod.

Napoleon's movements had completely puzzled his opponents and a council of war was summoned, but before any decision could be arrived at, two very important pieces of information came to hand. Some dispatches from the Emperor to Marie Louise fell into the hands of the Cossacks and were forwarded to headquarters ; one letter, dated the 22nd of March, stated that the army had crossed the Marne and that St Dizier had been occupied that evening.

Soon afterwards a courier from Count Pahlen arrived, announcing that the latter was in touch with Winzingerode, who formed the advance guard of the army of Silesia, and had already reached Vitry with some 8000 cavalry.

The Emperor's letter cleared up the situation considerably, for it was obvious that he was so far on the way to Chaumont that nothing could prevent him severing the communications of the Grand Army with Langres and the Upper Rhine. It was decided that the armies of Schwarzenberg and Blücher should effect their junction at Chalons and then continue the pursuit of Napoleon, basing themselves on Belgium, and the Emperor of Austria was warned to be prepared to leave Bar-sur-Aube at a moment's notice.

Meanwhile Blücher had somewhat recovered and resumed command, though he was still too weak to mount a horse and took the field in a barouche, while to protect his eyes from the sun, he had commandeered a lady's green silk bonnet. Bulow's corps had been sent to besiege Soissons, preparatory to advancing on Paris, while the remainder of the army commenced its march towards Reims on the 18th, with the intention of gaining touch with Schwarzenberg, through Chalons. Marmont, who had been left in command of the force detailed to contain Blücher, ordered Mortier to evacuate Reims and join him at Fismes. The two marshals then retreated to Chateau Thierry, followed by Yorck and Kleist, while Winzingerode, supported by Langeron and Sacken, marched along the main road to Chalons. Marmont crossed the Marne at Chateau Thierry, destroyed the bridge, and then marched through Montmirail towards Chalons, hoping to effect his junction with the Emperor at the latter town or at Vitry.

Meanwhile the French cavalry had captured a few convoys and completely disorganised Schwarzenberg's communications as far as Langres, besides which they had narrowly missed capturing the Emperor of Austria at Chaumont.

Napoleon, however, had changed his plans. He had succedeed in drawing the Allies from Paris, and he proposed to make for the Aube at Bar and open up communication with his capital through Troyes; therefore he recrossed to the left bank of the Marne at St Dizier and marched southward towards the Upper Aube. The situation on the night of the 24th was somewhat involved. Napoleon, marching south, had a rearguard under Macdonald at St Dizier; Ney was at Vassy, and the Emperor, with the Guard at Doulevant, with his cavalry out to the front towards Bar and Chaumont.

Marmont and Mortier were in the neighbourhood of Fere Champenoise, while Pacthod was at Vertus and a small detachment at Sezanne, all moving eastward to join the Emperor at Vitry.

Winzingerode, the vanguard of the army of Silesia, was on the right bank of the Marne between Vitry and St Dizier, while on the opposite bank of the river the main body of the Grand Army, consisting of the Guard, Reserve, 4th, 5th and 6th Corps, were concentrated west of the latter town, prepared to march on Chalons. The 3rd Corps was on the main road from Arcis to Chalons, midway between the former town and Sommesous, with a strong force of Russian cavalry, on its left, extending to the Aube at Plancy.

Of the army of Silesia, Woronzoff, with the infantry belonging to Winzingerode's corps, was between Chalons and Vitry; Langeron and Sacken had reached the former town, while Yorck and Kleist had succeeded in crossing the Marne and were between Chateau Thierry and Montmirail, following Marmont towards Chalons.

Thus in reality Schwarzenberg was marching away from Napoleon, to effect his junction with Blücher, leaving his opponent free to regain the main road to Paris at Bar, while if Marmont followed the Emperor's orders, he would inevitably be crushed between the various corps of the Grand Army and the army of Silesia, all of which were converging on the line of Chalons-Vitry.

A dispatch from Savary to the Emperor, setting forth the desperate state of affairs at Paris, had been captured by the Cossacks and forwarded to the Czar, who had reached Sommepuis early on the 24th. While he was carefully reviewing the situation, a courier arrived with dispatches announcing that Bordeaux had declared for Louis XVIII. and had been occupied by a detachment of the Anglo-Spanish army. The Czar decided that to continue the pursuit of Napoleon would merely cause the operations to drag on indefinitely, while a prompt advance on Paris in overwhelming force would bring the campaign to an immediate conclusion. He therefore summoned a council of war, consisting of De Tolly, Diebitsch and Toll, and, explaining the situation to them, asked their opinion. De Tolly was in favour of continuing the pursuit; Diebitsch, believing that Paris was the true objective, but not wishing to oppose his immediate superior, suggested sending Bulow's corps, some 50,000 strong, to the French capital and continuing the pursuit with the remainder of the united armies. Toll, however, pointed out that Bulow's force was too weak and might be crushed by Marmont and the various detachments of regular troops and National Guards in the neighbourhood of Paris. He advocated the immediate march of both armies on the hostile capital, while Winzingerode, with some 10,000 mounted troops, followed the Emperor, in order to lead him to suppose that he was still pursued by the Allied armies.

This bold proposition entirely coincided with the Czar's views, who at once rode towards Vitry to communicate his determination to the King of Prussia and Schwarzenberg. The former at once agreed, while Schwarzenberg, after some hesitation, realising that his communications with Switzerland were hopelessly interrupted, also gave his assent. Whereupon the Czar, rolling up the large map which he had used to demonstrate his views to his colleagues, exclaimed joyfully : " Let us all march to Paris."

CHAPTER VIII

THE FINAL ADVANCE ON PARIS

Blücher and Schwarzenberg march towards Paris—Winzingerode follows Napoleon—The French Cavalry cut the Communications of the Grand Army—Defeat of Marmont and Mortier at Fere Champenois—Napoleon defeats Winzingerode at St Dizier—The Allies cross the Marne at Meaux—Attack on Paris and Surrender of the City—Napoleon makes an Unsuccessful Attempt to reach his Capital — He is dethroned and abdicates

WHEN once the momentous resolution had been taken, the orders for the Grand Army to discontinue its pursuit of Napoleon and advance on Paris were promptly issued. During the afternoon Chernicheff, who commanded the advance guard of the army of Silesia, arrived at Vitry and was immediately granted an audience by the Czar. The Russian general earnestly advocated a general advance on the French capital, and was delighted when the Czar informed him that a decision to that effect had just been arrived at and the necessary orders already issued.

It was of the utmost importance that Napoleon, for a few days at least, should be kept in ignorance of the change in the plans of the Allied commanders, and for this purpose, Winzingerode, with some 8000 mounted troops and eight batteries of horse artillery, was ordered to continue the pursuit towards St Dizier. His instructions were to use every effort to mislead Napoleon and make him believe that the Grand Army was still following him, while he was also to report the Emperor's every movement to Schwarzenberg's headquarters. Chernicheff, with a large body of Cossacks, was to advance on his right, to watch the country between the Aube and the Upper Marne, while a small force was sent northward towards Metz, to give timely notice of any hostile movement in that direction.

The Grand Army and the army of Silesia were to advance on Paris by the most direct road and to effect their junction at Meaux. The former was to march via Fere Champenois and Sezanne, while the latter, from Chalons, was to move through Etoges and Montmirail.

This double line of advance would simplify the collection of supplies, which was a most serious question, as the rival armies had almost exhausted the resources of the district during the last two months, but the two portions of the Allied force would be within easy supporting distance of each other and there was only the detachments under Marmont and Mortier to bar their way to Paris.

It was indeed time that a resolute advance, with the whole available force, was commenced, for during the last two months the Allies had ceaselessly marched and countermarched from Troyes or Chalons towards the French capital and back again.

No longer hampered by Metternich, who had at last made up his mind that an accommodation with Napoleon was impossible, Schwarzenberg displayed a considerable share of firmness and energy.

Blücher was overjoyed at receiving a dispatch from his colleague couched in the most vigorous terms : " The enemy has marched by way of Vitry and St Dizier to cut our communications, therefore it has been decided to march on Paris with the full force of all the armies by the shortest route. I shall consequently, with all my troops, be at Fere Champenois on the 25th and at Meaux on the 28th, where I reckon positively on your Excellency's joining me with your entire force." [1]

As Nostitz remarks : " This coinciding of the decisions at main headquarters with what he himself considered wisest made the Field-Marshal very happy; all the more as it was the first time in the course of the two campaigns that such harmony had existed." [2]

---

[1] " Blücher," p. 248 (Heroes of the Nations Series, E. F. Henderson).

[2] *Ibid.*

At daybreak on the 25th of March, the Grand Army broke up from its bivouacs round Vitry and commenced its march towards Paris. The weather was dry and the roads had improved considerably, while the men were in the highest spirits at the news that they were to advance straight on the hostile capital, regardless of all obstacles.

Marmont and Mortier had received orders from the Emperor to join him and, totally ignorant of the changed plans of the Allies, were making their way towards Vitry. As a French detachment which had reoccupied Epernay had been driven from the town with heavy loss, the marshals had considered that the main road, along the southern bank of the Marne, was impassable, and decided to march by Etoges and Fere Champenois.

On the night of the 24th, they had bivouacked round Sommesous, and their advanced guard had already come in contact with the outposts of Wrede's corps, but though they could see the large circle of the watch fires of the hostile force, some eight miles to the east, they were still convinced that the main force of the Allies was following Napoleon.

Next morning all three armies resumed their march, Blücher's and Schwarzenberg's cavalry gaining touch some little distance east of Sommesous, while shortly afterwards Marmont's patrols

M

encountered the formidable mass of the Allied horsemen. Marmont immediately fell back to Sommesous and took up a defensive position in front of the village, at the same time sending an urgent message to Mortier to hasten to his support.

The latter, however, was already engaged with Blücher's cavalry, but managed to extricate himself and joined his colleague, whereupon both marshals fell back slowly towards Fere Champenois, harassed considerably by the hostile cavalry. The French force consisted of a little over 20,000 men, of whom nearly a quarter were cavalry, and 80 guns, while so far they had been engaged with a somewhat smaller number of mounted troops, who, however, had a considerable superiority of artillery.

The French horsemen at first strove gallantly to cover the retreat of their infantry, who were retiring in squares with admirable steadiness, but they were driven off by the more numerous hostile squadrons and some squares were then broken by a furious charge delivered by the Russian Chevalier Guard. Fresh bodies of hostile cavalry appeared on the flanks, and to make their situation still more desperate a furious rainstorm drove straight into the faces of the hard-pressed infantry and rendered the majority of their muskets useless. The French at last fell into disorder and poured through Fere

Champenois in confusion, but a gallant charge by a regiment of heavy cavalry temporarily checked the pursuit and Marmont seized the opportunity to re-form his men beyond the village.

Meanwhile a French division under Pacthod, escorting a large convoy of guns and supplies, had fallen in with Blücher's cavalry, as they were making their way to Vitry. Forming his men into squares to protect his convoy, Pacthod had offered a gallant resistance, but seeing that the day was going against him, he eventually abandoned his waggons and, harnessing the teams to his guns, retreated across the fields to Fere Champenois. Here he fell in with the remainder of the Allied cavalry, and though his 6000 men were almost entirely untrained conscripts, and he had only been able to bring off sixteen guns, he called upon his troops to resist to the last and prepared to cut his way through the masses of his opponents.

Retiring in squares, his gallant conscripts kept a steady fire, but though the Russian horse artillery tore great gaps in their ranks they still fought on gallantly, and repulsed several charges of the hostile cavalry.

The Czar sent an officer to the gallant Frenchman to beg him to surrender, as further resistance could only entail a purposeless loss of life, but Pacthod, returning a defiant answer, refused to yield.

The Russian guns were now brought up to close range and fired with deadly effect, while the whole of the cavalry fell furiously on the devoted squares, but the heroic conscripts fought doggedly on and over 3000 of them were cut down before the remainder would consent to lay down their arms. The gallant stand of Pacthod's division enabled Marmont to draw off almost unmolested, but nevertheless over 7000 prisoners, 80 guns, 2000 waggons of ammunition and an enormous convoy of stores fell into the hands of the Allies, at a cost of under 2500 casualties.

The action is remarkable from the fact that the Allied cavalry alone were engaged, though they were supported by a formidable force of horse artillery, and they succeeded in defeating a force of all arms, containing a large proportion of veteran troops.

Marmont had now only some 12,000 men and 40 guns, consequently he could only manœuvre to check the enemy's advance, but was nearly cut off at La Ferte Gaucher, as part of Kleist's corps had anticipated him by seizing the town, while Pahlen was pressing hard on his rearguard.

Fortunately for the French, the Crown Prince of Wurtemberg interfered and checked Pahlen's advance, so that the French were eventually able to reach Provins. Pahlen, however, still followed them relentlessly, and at the sight of his Cossacks they hurriedly abandoned Provins and retreated through Nangis and Guignes towards Paris.

Meanwhile the Grand Army and the army of Silesia marched unmolested along the main road to Meaux, the men in the highest spirits, as the weather had at last cleared and the roads were in excellent condition.

Winzingerode meanwhile was in touch with the strong hostile rearguard under Macdonald, but he carried out his instructions so thoroughly that for two or three days the latter was convinced that he was followed by the whole of the Grand Army.

The approach of detachments of French mounted troops sent the Emperor and his entourage of diplomatists in hot haste from Chaumont to Dijon, and the panic spread to the frontier, where it was believed that the Allies had been utterly overwhelmed and that Napoleon was in full march to the Rhine. However, as Macdonald reported that he had only encountered cavalry, the Emperor became uneasy and ordered his troops to concentrate and rendezvous at St Dizier.

Winzingerode had meanwhile occupied the latter town, giving out that the main body would shortly arrive and sent forward Tettenborn, with some 3000 men, to follow up the enemy.

The latter, realising that the whole French force was advancing against him, commenced to retreat, while Winzingerode drew up his 5000 mounted troops in front of St Dizier to cover the retirement of his advance guard.

The French, in overwhelming numbers, pressed forward with the greatest vigour, and Tettenborn, cutting his way through the hostile cavalry with the greatest difficulty, managed to reach Vitry, though not without heavy loss. The storm then burst on Winzingerode's men, who were driven from their position in confusion and only saved from complete disaster by a gallant stand made by their rear-guard on the road to Bar-le-Duc. Winzingerode managed to re-form his shaken troops, but was forced to evacuate the latter town and continue his retreat to Chalons, with a loss of nearly 2000 men, including prisoners, and 9 guns.

Napoleon, inspirited by his brilliant little success, determined to make another attempt on Vitry, and brought over 100 guns into action against the town, but learning from the prisoners that Winzingerode's force was composed of only mounted troops, and from some peasants that Marmont had been heavily defeated at Fere Champenois, he abandoned the siege and fell back to St Dizier.

He at last realised that he had been followed only

by a comparatively weak detachment, while the main body of the Allies was well on its way to Paris. He spent the night in studying maps and carefully considering the situation, which filled him with the most gloomy forebodings ; it was obvious that his plans had been frustrated by the unexpected energy and determination of his opponents and that operations against their communications would no longer produce the slightest effect. He determined to give up his idea of basing himself on the fortresses of the Rhine provinces and return to Paris by the southern road through Troyes, Sens and Fontainebleau, but the Allies, who were moving by the more direct route, had gained a start of three clear days, and it was doubtful whether he could rejoin the marshals before the capital surrendered. His dash at the hostile communications had produced little permanent effect, for General Ertel, who commanded the posts in rear of the Grand Army, had taken his measures with the greatest promptitude and not only withdrawn the bulk of the stores to Langres but, joined by some reinforcements from the Rhine, had prevented the inhabitants interrupting the communications, and maintained order in rear of the army.

On the 27th, the advanced guard of the army of Silesia had driven a small French force from Meaux and thrown some temporary bridges across the

Marne, while next day the leading columns of the Allies commenced to cross to the right bank. The Czar took the opportunity of reviewing Sacken's corps, and personally thanked them for the gallantry they had displayed since the commencement of the campaign. The compliment was fully deserved, for of the 20,000 who had crossed the Rhine three months previously, only some 6000 remained with the colours.

The Czar also issued the most stringent orders against pillage, and forbade the requisition of supplies, except through the local authorities, who were to be promptly settled with, and his humane instructions were, on the whole, faithfully carried out.

A certain amount of delay had occurred owing to the fact that both armies crossed the Marne in the neighbourhood of Meaux, and this enabled the marshals to complete their circuitous march through Guignes and interpose between the Allies and Paris. For years Napoleon had intended to surround his capital with an adequate girdle of fortifications but had refrained, principally from the fear of alarming the Parisians, and though he had issued orders on the subject at the end of the preceding year, nothing had been accomplished. Consequently chaos reigned in the city. The wildest rumours were afloat. The Jacobins gave out that the Allies intended to burn Paris and banish the inhabitants, and urged the citizens to resist to the last. On the 29th, Joseph published an inspiring manifesto, stating that Napoleon was hastening to the relief of the city with a large army and encouraging the citizens to hold out until his arrival, while the Czar issued a proclamation setting forth that the Allies only made war against Napoleon and not against the French nation.

Marmont had assumed the direction of affairs, for though Mortier was the senior marshal, he was merely a hard-fighting soldier, and being without a trace of petty jealousy in his composition, he was completely dominated by his brilliant junior.

Including the National Guard and conscripts hurried up from the neighbouring depots, there were only some 35,000 men available for the defence of the city, but a certain number of officials, pensioners and the students of the military schools were also requisitioned, and 150 guns, some of the largest calibre, with a plentiful supply of ammunition, were available.

At 2 A.M. on the morning of the 30th of March, the drums beat the *generale* throughout Paris, and the National Guard, assembling hastily, marched to their appointed positions.

The Allied troops were also under arms before

dawn, and soon after daybreak, heavy columns were seen approaching on the road from Meaux.

Raeffskoi's Russian corps, supported by the reserves under De Tolly, were to attack the French centre between Pantin and Vincennes, their especial object being to sieze the heights of Belleville, while the Prince of Wurtemberg's corps, supported by Gyulai, was to advance on their left, clear the forest of Vincennes and then attack the bridges over the Marne at Charenton and St Maur. The army of Silesia had been intended to co-operate in the attack by advancing against Montmartre from St Denis and Le Bourget, but, thanks to the incompetence of the Austrian staff, the orders were not received at the headquarters of the army of Silesia in sufficient time for Blücher to make his dispositions overnight, and consequently it was after midday before he was able to join in the attack.

About six o'clock, Eugene of Wurtemberg, with a Russian division, advanced from Pantin, while Raeffskoi, on his left, moved forward towards the heights round Romanville, with Pahlen's dragoons on his outer flank.

Marmont at once realised that the villages should have been held, and advanced along the plateau, with Boyer's division of the Young Guard, to occupy them. As Eugene was also advancing, a furious combat ensued, eventually spreading as far as Romanville. Finding that no immediate attack was to be apprehended on Montmartre, Mortier now sent a couple of divisions to support Marmont, and after a desperate struggle, Eugene's division was driven back to Pantin, with the loss of 1500 men.

He sent an urgent message to De Tolly, stating that, while prepared to die at his post, he could not hold the village much longer without support, but Raeffskoi was now coming into action on his left against Romanville, while Pahlen had worked round the hostile right and was threatening the rear of the Young Guard from Charrone.

The Czar, arriving on the field about eight o'clock, immediately took in the situation, and ordered De Tolly to bring forward the whole of the reserve to support Eugene's hard-pressed division round Pantin.

Three divisions of Russian Guards also advanced to support Raeffskoi, and after a desperate struggle the French were forced to abandon the high ground round Romanville and fall back to the heights of Belleville at the western extremity of the plateau.

Pahlen meanwhile had pushed a detachment of his dragoons through Vincennes and captured a battery of 20 guns, manned by the Polytechnic students, outside the Barrière du Trone.

Marmont had been driven back to the Belleville
heights and the Russian columns had formed up
opposite his position, but De Tolly ordered them to
suspend their advance, as neither the army of Silesia,
on the right, nor the Prince of Wurtemberg's corps,
on the left, had yet come into action.   About eleven
o'clock, the columns of Blücher's army were seen
to be approaching Montmartre ; Kleist and Yorck
advancing along the main road from St Denis, with
Langeron on their right, threatening the extreme
left of the French position.

A desperate and prolonged struggle took place for
the possession of the villages of La Chapelle and Le
Villette, and it was not until Woronzoff brought up a
division of Russian infantry to support the Prussians
that the French were driven from the villages.

Marmont, who had meanwhile received some
reinforcements, now made an attempt to recapture
Pantin, but De Tolly sent forward the Prussian and
Baden Guard and, after a sharp struggle, the French
were driven back in confusion.

About one o'clock, Wurtemberg's corps made its
tardy appearance on the left of the line and, pushing
through the forest of Vincennes without encountering any opposition, captured the bridge of St Maur
and drove the French, with heavy loss, back to
Charenton.

The Czar now ordered a general attack against the whole front of the hostile position, Langeron was ordered to carry the ridge of Montmartre, regardless of cost, while Raeffskoi and De Tolly pressed forward along the plateau against Marmont's position at Belleville.

Though the French troops, regulars and National Guard alike, fought with the utmost heroism, the situation was hopeless, for the Allies had nearly 100,000 men in action. The outlying villages were carried at the point of the bayonet and the Allied columns converged on Belleville, the men cheering wildly as they beheld Paris spread out at their feet.

Suddenly the advance was checked and the victorious troops brought to a standstill, for, seeing that the city itself was in danger of being stormed, Joseph had sent an officer to the Czar to request an armistice.

The latter replied that the only terms he would accept were the immediate surrender of Paris and the withdrawal of the French troops within the barrier. An officer was sent to seek Marmont, who was found in the thick of the fight at Belleville, encouraging his men, and orders to cease fire were immediately issued, but the fight still raged furiously round Montmartre. Langeron's attack against the extreme left of the French position had at last been successful, and a sudden wild outburst of cheering was heard, as the Russian colours topped the ridge of Montmartre.

The desperate character of the fighting was shown by the fact that the Allies lost close on 10,000 men, no less than 7000 of whom were Russians, while the French losses amounted to about 4500.

The heavy casualties sustained by the Allies were due not so much to the fact that the French defended their positions with the most obstinate gallantry or to the fire of the hostile artillery as to Schwarzenberg's incompetence and the gross mismanagement of his staff, which caused Raeffskoi to make an entirely unsupported attack on the French centre for several hours, thus failing to utilise their great numerical superiority.

Napoleon had pushed on with frenzied haste towards his capital, leaving his Guard at Troyes. He entered his travelling carriage in the early hours of the 30th, and ceaselessly urged his postilions to increase their pace.

Disastrous tidings met him at every stage, but he still pushed recklessly forward and arrived at Fromenteau, fifteen miles from Paris, at 10 P.M., but here he met General Belliard, who informed him that the city had capitulated.

Napoleon then abandoned himself to a frenzy of rage, heaping unstinted abuse upon Joseph, Marmont and his generals, even making wild plans for re-capturing the city, as soon as his troops arrived.

Meanwhile there had been some difficulty in arranging the terms of capitulation, but the Czar was in a generous mood and eventually the two marshals and the regular troops were allowed to march out, while the National Guard was to remain to keep order in the city.

Shortly after eight o'clock the Allied monarchs made their triumphant entry into Paris, and received a most enthusiastic reception from the populace, who were delighted with the imposing cortège and the magnificent appearance of the Russian and Prussian Guards.

Now that the object of his ambition was an accomplished fact, Blücher, who had mounted his horse and taken part in the final attack on Montmartre, relapsed into the moody lethargy from which he had suffered since his breakdown after the battle of Laon, and absolutely refused to enter Paris with the Allied monarchs. At the brilliant review of the combined armies, later in the day, the King of Prussia expressed strong disapprobation at the ragged state of the army of Silesia, and requested Yorck to look at the Prussian Guards. That uncompromising general, however, pointed to war-worn veterans, who had marched and fought under Blücher since

the commencement of the campaign, and replied:
" Your Majesty, those are your guards."

On the 2nd of April, the Senate dethroned the
Emperor and appointed a provisional Government,
to which, after some correspondence with Schwarzenberg, Marmont finally gave his adherence, and his
corps, still nearly 12,000 strong, encamped at
Versailles, preparatory to marching into Normandy,
where it had been decided that it should be quartered
for the present.

Meanwhile Napoleon remained at Fontainebleau,
nursing wild schemes for attempting the recapture
of Paris, but though the rank and file as well as a
large number of the junior officers were ready to
follow him anywhere, Ney, Macdonald and the
senior generals were bitterly opposed to his rash
projects, which would only have entailed much useless bloodshed and could have achieved no useful
result.

The matter was finally settled, however, by the
news that the Senate had deposed the Emperor,
and after a conference at which Ney, Macdonald,
Lefebvre, Oudinot, Berthier and Bertrand were
present, Napoleon bowed to the inevitable and signed
his abdication.

CHAPTER IX

THE PROGRESS OF THE CAMPAIGN IN THE SUBSIDIARY THEATRES OF WAR

Wellington's Operations in the South-West of France—The Passage of the Adour—The Battle of Orthez—The Occupation of Bordeaux—The Battle of Toulouse—Augereau's Operations in the Valley of the Rhone—Advance of the Allies—Augereau assumes the Offensive—His Feeble Strategy—The Allies again advance—The Battle of Limonet and Occupation of Lyons—Eugene's Operations in Northern Italy—Action on the Mincio—Defeat of Murat—The Capture of Genoa—Operations in the Netherlands—Winzingerode crosses the Rhine—Graham and Bulow invest Antwerp—The Siege abandoned—Failure of Graham's Attempt to capture Bergen-op-Zoom—Maison retreats to the Frontier

Operations of the Anglo-Spanish Army under the Duke of Wellington in the South-West of France.— By the middle of December 1813, when the unusually inclement weather forced the Duke of Wellington to suspend operations and distribute his army in winter quarters, he had crossed the Pyrenees, forced the passage of the Nive and Nivelle, and firmly established himself in the extreme south-west corner of France. The excellent discipline he enforced amongst his troops encouraged the country people to bring supplies to the camps of the Allies, while the undisputed command of the sea enjoyed by the British navy enabled him to base himself on Irun and the neighbouring Spanish ports.

Consequently, though the shortage of ready money was a continual source of worry, and the troops were for the most part clothed in rags, the Allies suffered little from the difficulty usually experienced in feeding a large army in hostile territory. It was far otherwise with Soult, who had concentrated his force in the entrenched camps under the guns of Bayonne and who was so lamentably short of ready money that he was compelled to allow his troops to levy forced contributions on the surrounding districts, thus intensifying the hostility of the inhabitants, amongst whom a strong feeling in favour of the restoration of the Bourbons already existed.

It was not until the middle of February 1814 that the weather became sufficiently open to permit Wellington resuming active operations, and he then brought up his cavalry, who had wintered in the valley of the Ebro, and prepared to carry out his advance into the heart of France.

The rival leaders were singularly well matched. Both were strategists of the highest order, quick to form their plans and resolute in carrying them out, but on the actual field of battle the French marshal was slightly inferior to his great opponent, for he not infrequently displayed a certain hesitation at the critical moment, when a little additional energy would have ensured the success of his carefully laid plans. He also suffered from a slight inferiority of force, as he had only some 70,000 men to oppose to the 100,000 under the British general, while his troops were of considerably less fighting value, as, though he had a large number of veterans of the Peninsular campaigns still with the colours, he had been ordered to send large drafts to the Emperor and to Augereau, while the conscripts who took their place were only partially trained and had little enthusiasm for the struggle.

As soon as Wellington showed a disposition to resume the offensive, Soult left a garrison of some 10,000 men in Bayonne and concentrated the remainder of his force to his left, round St Juan Pied-de-Port.

Wellington's plan was to force the passage of the Adour near its mouth and mask the powerful fortress of Bayonne, but he intended first of all to distract Soult's attention from the proposed movement by a vigorous attack on the French centre and left. On the 14th of February, Hill drove back the hostile outposts and invested St Juan Pied-de-Port, while

Beresford forced the centre, under Clausel, to fall back behind the Gave de Mauleon.

Meanwhile Hope made careful preparations for the passage of the Adour between Bayonne and its mouth, and carried out the difficult operation, with little loss, on the morning of the 23rd of February.

His success was in a great measure due to the invaluable co-operation of the navy, under Admiral Penrose, for though a heavy sea was running, and a severe north-westerly gale blowing, the boats of the warships forced their way across the bar in the most gallant manner, though unfortunately the lives of many sailors were sacrificed in the dangerous operation.

Soult had meanwhile left a garrison in St Juan Pied-de-Port and fallen back to the neighbourhood of Sauveterre, whence he could cover the points of passage over the Gave d'Oleron. He again retreated for a short distance and posted his force, some 40,000 strong, on the heights north of the Gave de Pau, with his left resting on the town of Orthez. Wellington advanced against the formidable position in three columns and commenced his attack soon after nine o'clock on the morning of Sunday the 27th. At first he met with little success. Beresford, on the extreme left, was brought to a standstill opposite St

Boes, while Picton's assault on the right centre of the French position was repulsed with heavy loss. For a moment Soult's star appeared to be in the ascendant, and the marshal exclaimed with delight : " At last I have him ! " but Wellington had already taken his measures to restore the fight and, after a desperate struggle, the heroic constancy of the British infantry once again triumphed. Soult conducted his retreat with considerable skill, and eventually rallied his troops behind the Luy de Bearn, though he had been severely hustled by Hill, who had crossed the Gave de Pau above Orthez and taken up the pursuit with great vigour. Wellington himself had been slightly wounded during the action and the losses had been severe, the Allies losing some 2000 killed and wounded, while the French casualties amounted to nearly 4000, and in addition a large number of conscripts deserted the colours and returned to their homes. Soult continued his retreat towards St Sever, breaking down the bridges over the mountain torrents to retard pursuit, and eventually moved eastward along both banks of the Adour, thus keeping the foothills of the Pyrenees on his right and facilitating his junction with Suchet, who had already commenced to abandon Catalonia.

Wellington followed him along the right bank of the Adour and sent a detachment of some 12,000 men to occupy Bordeaux, where the sentiment in favour of the Bourbons had manifested itself most unmistakably.

On the 2nd of March, Hill gained a brilliant little victory over Clausel, who, with Villate's and Harispe's divisions, had been sent to remove stores accumulated at Aire, but Wellington was unable to follow up the victory with effect, as he had only some 27,000 men available, a large proportion of his force being employed in the investment of Bayonne and St Juan Pied-de-Port as well as in the expedition to Bordeaux. Soult made an attempt to assume the offensive, but hearing that Bordeaux had actually been occupied by the Allies, he abandoned his project and fell back to Tarbes, sending a large body of conscripts, who had proved anything but reliable, direct to Toulouse, where he intended to make a final stand. On the 19th, sharp actions took place at Vic-Bigorre and outside Tarbes, but the French were again defeated, whereupon Soult retreated to Toulouse and, after a magnificent forced march, reached the latter city on the 25th of March.

Hampered by his numerous artillery and pontoon train, Wellington only appeared before the city two days later, and was still further delayed by the flooded state of the Garonne. He had meanwhile been rejoined by Beresford, who had left a small garrison in Bordeaux, and at first intended to cross the Garonne above Toulouse, so as to prevent Soult effecting his junction with Suchet.

Hill, with two divisions and Morillo's Spaniards, crossed to the northern bank of the river, but the continual rain had made the roads impassable, and he eventually returned to the left bank. Balked in his original intention, Wellington now determined to cross some fifteen miles below the town, and Beresford, with about 15,000 men, was transferred to the right bank, but a sudden flood necessitated the removal of the pontoons and he remained isolated for three days. Soult, however, made no attempt to profit by the mishap, and contented himself with strengthening his already formidable position; he erected several powerful redoubts on the Calvinet ridge, which commanded the city from the north and fortified the bridges over the Languedoc Canal.

On the morning of the 8th, Wellington was able to repair the bridges, and transferred the remainder of his force, with the exception of two divisions under Hill, to the northern bank. The French position was an extremely strong one, and Soult had used the respite afforded him to the best possible advantage; his main position was on the Calvinet ridge, while the city itself was surrounded on the northwest and south by the Languedoc Canal and the

Garonne. After a careful reconnaisance, Wellington decided to attack the ridge and make a feint at the bridges over the canal, west of the town, while Hill attacked the suburb of St Ciprien, south of the Garonne.

A brilliant little skirmish at Croix d'Orate, which resulted in the 18th Hussars defeating the French cavalry and seizing the bridge over the Ers, enabled the Allies to approach Toulouse from the west, and the stage was set for the final battle of the Peninsular War.

Wellington actually brought about 52,000 men into the field, but nearly a quarter of his force consisted of Spanish troops, while Soult had some 38,000 men, though a large proportion of them were conscripts who had but little stomach for the fight.

At 2 A.M. on Easter Sunday, the 10th of April, the Allies stood to arms, and as soon as it was light, Picton drove in the French outposts and advanced against the western extremity of the ridge, followed by the Light Division and Freyre's Spaniards. Picton and the Light Division then moved off to their right, to attack the bridges over the Languedoc Canal, while the Spaniards occupied Pujade, an isolated hill on the west of the Calvinet ridge, and Hill commenced his advance against St Ciprien. Beresford, with the 4th and 6th Divisions, had been ordered to march along the front of the French position between the foot of the Calvinet Slope and the Ers and then wheel to his right and establish himself on the ridge and overwhelm the hostile right.

His march was an exceedingly dangerous one, as he was under artillery fire for nearly two miles and the ground was so swampy that he was unable to take his guns with him; moreover, he was liable at any moment to be vigorously attacked on his right flank.

The Spaniards now made a somewhat rash attack on the redoubts on the western edge of the Calvinet ridge, and were repulsed with crushing loss and pursued for some distance by the hostile infantry. The situation was critical in the extreme. Beresford was already committed to his long flank march; Picton had been severely repulsed in his attempt to force the bridge at Jumeau, and Hill, after making considerable progress, was temporarily brought to a standstill in front of St Ciprien. There were now reserves available, and the French pursuit was only checked by the steadiness of some battalions of the Light Division, who coolly changed front left and smote the hostile infantry in flank with several deadly volleys, forcing them to return precipitately to their former position. Everything now depended on the success of Beresford's movement, and just as he was about to wheel to his right, Soult launched a vigorous counterstroke; luckily it was delivered a few minutes too late and the leading British regiments had time to deploy. Their deadly fire checked the French and a determined bayonet charge finally drove them up the slope in confusion and enabled Beresford to establish himself firmly on the ridge. It was about three o'clock when he gave the signal to advance, and the 4th and 6th Divisions swept forward against the French centre; two redoubts were captured with a rush by the Highland Brigade, but the French rallied and a desperate struggle took place. The 42nd especially covered themselves with glory, and lost more than half their strength in the furious hand-to-hand fighting, but the French were eventually driven back in confusion. Soult now withdrew his men into the town and took up his position behind the canal, but darkness had already fallen and neither side was capable of further effort. Next day Wellington determined to allow his men a much-needed rest and to replenish his ammunition before commencing the final attack on the city, but during the night Soult skilfully withdrew his troops and marched off to Carcassonne to join Suchet.

The losses were very heavy, the bulk occurring among the Spaniards and the 4th and 6th Divisions, whose heroic courage and constancy had alone rendered the victory possible. Wellington entered the city on the morning of the 12th of April and received an ovation from the inhabitants, most of whom had already mounted the " White Cockade," though the news of Napoleon's abdication did not arrive until late in the evening. Soult had been aware that Paris had already fallen and that the Emperor was in desperate straits, but did not know that he had already abdicated, so, like the gallant soldier that he was, he determined to fight to the last.

The Operations of Marshal Augereau in the Valley of the Rhone.—Towards the end of December 1813, Count Bubna, whose corps formed the extreme left wing of the Grand Army, advanced from Geneva into the valley of the Upper Rhone. His progress was so slow, however, that it was nearly a month later when he approached Lyons, and, unaware of the weakness of the garrison, he fell back to Montleul and divided his corps, sending one detachment to overrun Savoy and another towards Chalons-sur-Soane to collect supplies.

Augereau meanwhile had arrived at Lyons with reinforcements, and had been further strengthened by a large draft of veteran troops from Suchet's army. The Emperor intended him to drive back Bubna and act with vigour against Schwarzenberg's communications, but Augereau entirely failed to appreciate the situation and divided his force. The detachment under Marchand recaptured Chambery and the Echelles defile, but he himself only advanced as far as Bourg. Napoleon was by no means satisfied with these feeble operations, which produced no effect in the main theatre of operations, and wrote urging the marshal to forget that he was fifty-six years old and to think only of the days of Castiglione. Shortly afterwards Berthier wrote : " The Emperor is not satisfied with your dispositions, in pushing detachments in this manner wherever the enemy has forces, instead of striking at his heart. He directs me in consequence to reiterate the orders you have already three times received. You are to unite all your forces into one column and march either into the Pays de Vaud or the Jura, according as the enemy is in the most force in one or the other. It is by concentrating forces in masses that great successes are obtained." [1]

Instead of acting on these clear instructions, which should have been unnecessary to a general of his standing, Augereau continued his aimless operations, and grumbled ceaselessly at the quality of his troops. The Emperor made great efforts to reinforce him and

[1] Alison, " History of Europe," vol. xi.

Suchet was ordered to send a further large draft of veterans, while Eugene was also instructed to send some troops from Italy. The only result, however, was that Marchand drove Bubna into Geneva, but shortly afterwards Augereau was obliged to concentrate his detachments for the defence of Lyons, as the newly formed " Army of the South " was advancing into the valley of the Rhone. After an unsuccessful attempt to recapture Mâcon, Augereau retreated down the left bank of the Rhone but determined to make one last attempt to save Lyons. He consequently took up his position at Limonet, but was attacked and defeated by Hesse-Homburg on the 19th and 20th of March; he then abandoned Lyons and fell back to Valence, eventually taking up his position behind the Isere. He now learned that the Allies had occupied Bordeaux and was ordered to send the majority of the veterans he had received from Suchet to reinforce Soult, and abandoning the line of the Isere, he distributed his disheartened troops along the right bank of the Rhone in order to prevent Hesse-Homburg working round his flank and gaining touch with the Anglo-Spanish force on the Upper Garrone.

Marshal Suchet's Operations in Catalonia.—The large drafts that he was ordered to send to Soult and Augereau reduced Suchet's field army to about 20,000 men, consequently he was too weak to undertake any important operations against the Spanish and Anglo-Sicilian forces whch hemmed him in against the Pyrenees. The French still held several fortresses, though, with the exception of Barcelona and Figueras, they were of little importance and the garrisons would have been much more usefully employed with the field army, but Napoleon consistently refused to abandon a single inch of territory. Eventually Suchet was ordered to send a second strong draft to Augereau and, evacuating Gerona and leaving Barcelona to its face, he withdrew the garrisons from the other fortresses and concentrated the remainder of his sadly diminished force round Figueras.

Here he remained until Ferdinand's return to Spain, when he retreated across the Pyrenees and endeavoured to join Soult but the armistice was declared before he could accomplish his object.

Eugene's Operations in Northern Italy.—At the commencement of the campaign of 1814, Eugene was on the defensive behind the Adige, with an army largely composed of untrained Italian conscripts, though he also had a weak French division and a stiffening of veteran officers and non-commissioned officers drawn from Suchet's army.

His troubles were increased by Murat's doubtful

attitude, and when the latter finally threw in his lot with the Allies, Eugene was obliged to abandon the line of the Adige and retire behind the Mincio.

On the 8th of February, by a strange coincidence, both Eugene and the Austrian commander, Bellegarde, determined to assume the offensive, and a confused struggle on both banks of the river, in which neither side gained any material advantage, resulted. Eugene then sent his least reliable troops into garrison at Mantua and Peschiera, and concentrated the remainder on the Po, so as to be able to act on either bank of the river at will.

Murat now made some pretence of co-operating with Bellegarde and advanced to the Po, but his Neapolitan troops proved absolutely worthless and were heavily defeated by Grenier's French division.

Bellegarde's plans were completely upset by the impossibility of relying on Murat, who, fearing that the Allies intended to restore the Bourbons to the throne of Naples, was meditating rejoining the Emperor and was in secret correspondence with Eugene. With the exception of the capture of Genoa by an Anglo-Sicilian expedition under Lord William Bentinck, nothing of importance occurred in Northern Italy until the news of Napoleon's abdication was received, when Eugene promptly concluded an armistice with the Austrian commander by which

French troops were allowed to return to their own country.

The Operations in the Netherlands.—At the commencement of 1814, Bergen-op-Zoom was the only important Dutch fortress remaining in French hands, while Count Maison's force was so weak that, after furnishing garrisons for the more important Belgian fortresses, he was only able to observe the powerful Allied corps under Bulow and Winzingerode. Bernadotte should have taken the field in person with a cosmopolitan force some 170,000 strong, but he never had the least intention of taking part in the operations and at the commencement of the campaign was engaged in quarrelling with the Danes over the question of the occupation of Norway.

A British corps some 10,000 strong, under the command of Sir Thomas Graham, had been sent to Holland with the intention of seizing Antwerp, as that important naval base was one of the main points of contention between Great Britain and Napoleon. Early in January, Winzingerode forced the passage of the Rhine near Düsseldorf and advanced to the Meuse, eventually capturing the important fortresses of Liège and Namur, but his operations then came to a temporary standstill, as his field force was seriously reduced by the number of troops he was forced to employ to guard his communications.

About the middle of January Graham and Bulow advanced towards Antwerp and drove in the French outpost after a sharp skirmish at Merxem. They then proceeded to bombard the city, but their artillery was too weak to produce any material effect. Bulow was then ordered to advance towards the French frontier, and as Graham was too weak to continue the siege, he retired to Tholen. The defence of Antwerp was notable from the fact that Carnot, who had been living in retirement in Switzerland since Napoleon's accession to power, offered his services to his country in her hour of need and had been appointed governor of the important fortress, which was one of the Emperor's most cherished possessions.

The Duke of Saxe-Weimar, with a corps composed of detachments from the lesser German states, had, meanwhile, driven Maison back to the shelter of the fortresses guarding the French frontier but had been unable to obtain any material success. On the 8th of March, Graham made an attempt to capture the important fortress of Bergen-op-Zoom by a *coup de main*, but though his plans were carefully laid and the storming parties succeeded in establishing themselves on the ramparts with little loss, they were left without support, and the attempt ended in a most disastrous failure, entailing a loss of over 2500 men, including prisoners.

o

Bulow and Winzingerode had, meanwhile, marched to join Blücher on the Marne, and though Maison was too weak to take the field against Saxe-Weimar, he managed to hold his ground under the guns of the frontier fortresses until the news of Napoleon's abdication brought the campaign to an end.

The comparative failure of the operations in the Netherlands was entirely due to Bernadotte's selfishness, as, had he taken the field at the commencement of the campaign with his whole available force, he must have crushed Maison and could then have co-operated with great effect in the invasion of France.

In reviewing the events of the short but momentous campaign, the impartial observer cannot fail to be struck by the courage and determination displayed by the Emperor in continuing the hopeless struggle against the overwhelming forces of the coalition. The two previous campaigns had ended in the most disastrous fashion, and the former invincibility of his arms was clearly a thing of the past, while the resources of France were completely exhausted and the people were bitterly opposed to the continuance of the struggle. The Emperor's most urgent needs were time to reorganise the resources of the country and men to fill the depleted ranks of his armies.

To a certain extent, he obtained the former, thanks to the procrastination of his opponents and the extreme difficulty they experienced in framing a plan of campaign which should satisfy the conflicting ambitions of the various nations forming the coalition. The difficulty of obtaining sufficient recruits, however, proved insurmountable, and the great numerical inferiority of his forces constantly robbed the Emperor of the fruits of his victories and prevented his profiting to the full by the blunders of his opponents.

He was never sufficiently strong to enable him to leave an adequate force to contain one of the hostile armies while he dealt with the other; in fact, both his striking and containing forces were necessarily so weak that he was unable to follow up his successes but was forced to hurry back to support the detachments he had left to retard the advance of either Blücher or Schwarzenberg. Had the latter been a more enterprising leader, even Napoleon's genius could not have prolonged the campaign, but divided councils, political considerations and the want of a strong supreme commander to control the movements of both armies paralysed the strategy of the Allies.

Even in quality, the bulk of the French troops were markedly inferior to their opponents, for though the Guard and the veterans of the Peninsular campaign under Soult and Suchet were unsurpassed by any soldiers of that period, the remaining regiments were principally composed of partially trained conscripts, who had most unwillingly been forced into the ranks.

That the Emperor was able to inspire these raw and badly equipped troops, and to achieve such astonishing results with such unpromising material, is surely one of the most marked manifestations of his genius as a commander.

It has sometimes been urged that he did not employ even his available force to the best advantage, but, with the exception of Suchet's veteran troops in Catalonia, this criticism does not appear to have been justified by the conditions under which the campaign was fought.

The fact that Davout and some 50,000 French troops were shut up in Hamburg and other fortresses throughout Germany was an unavoidable legacy from the previous campaign, which the Emperor was powerless to remedy. It is true that they served no useful purpose, as they did not even prevent an equal number of their opponents taking part in the operations in the main theatre of war but were for the most part blockaded and forced to surrender by the least efficient of the Prussian Landwehr, who were quite unfit to take the field, or by detachments of the Russian reserves on their way to the front.

From a purely military point of view, Soult's

project of leaving a strong detachment in the Pyrenees under Clausel to act against the communications of the Anglo-Spanish force, whilst he himself marched to join the Emperor, with the remainder of his army, was by no means a bad one.

However, the strong feeling in favour of the Bourbons, which had already manifested itself in the south-west of France, would have rendered this move nothing less than an abandonment of the whole country south of the Garonne, while the local National Guard were so disaffected that they could not have been depended on to offer any opposition to Wellington's advance.

In Northern Italy, the bulk of Eugene's force was composed of locally raised conscripts, who would most certainly have refused to serve outside their own country, but, stiffened by a small proportion of French troops, they succeeded in preventing the 50,000 men under Bellegarde taking any part in the invasion of France. Maison's weak force also achieved its object, for to a certain extent it delayed the advance of Bulow and Winzingerode, while it prevented the German corps under Saxe-Weimar taking any part in the operations in the main theatre of war.

The one fatal mistake appears to have been the Emperor's determination to retain his hold on

Catalonia as long as possible, but this was dictated by political rather than by military considerations.

The determination never to abandon an inch of territory that he had already occupied was one of Napoleon's most marked characteristics, and, as a rule, it was dictated by sound common-sense.   For since 1805 the French armies had been largely reinforced by contingents drawn from the vassal states, and this had been especially noticeable in 1812, when a large proportion of the " Grande Armée " was composed of troops drawn from Italy and the smaller German states.

Thus the territories actually occupied by Napoleon formed recruiting areas for his armies and were denied to his opponents, but this reason hardly applied to Catalonia, as the spirit of the population was so bitterly hostile that few of the Spaniards ever served in the ranks of the French army.

The defence of the frontier might safely have been left to the local National Guard, as the Allied forces in the north-eastern corner of Spain were so lacking in training and organisation that they would have been incapable of any serious offensive movement.   Had Suchet been ordered to withdraw his garrisons, he could have concentrated some 50,000 veteran troops of excellent quality and have effectively co-operated with Soult in opposing Wellington, but his force was so weakened by the continual drafts that he was ordered to send to Soult and Augereau that he was unable to take any useful part in the campaign. The appointment of Augereau to command the force assembling round Lyons was an inexplicable error, as even at his best that marshal had been nothing but an energetic and hard-fighting divisional general, and of late years he had entirely lost all his former vigour and degenerated into a useless grumbler. Napoleon's choice seems the more strange as he had, with justice, been profoundly disgusted by the incompetence and lack of enterprise displayed by the marshal in the fighting round Leipzig in the previous autumn. Could the Emperor have made up his mind to abandon Catalonia, and had he transferred Suchet, with the bulk of his veteran troops, to the valley of the Rhone, the course of the campaign might have been materially altered. For Suchet was undoubtedly quite one of the ablest of the marshals, and, besides being a thoroughly capable commander and organiser, had the knack of getting the most out of young and partially trained troops.

With a force composed of conscripts and veterans, in almost equal proportions, he would undoubtedly have succeeded in creating a most effective diversion by a sustained and vigorous attack on the communications of Schwarzenberg's army, probably causing the latter to beat a precipitate retreat to the Rhine. Though the majority of the marshals were undoubtedly averse to the continuation of the struggle, yet, with the exception of Augereau, they undoubtedly served the Emperor to the best of their ability, while Soult and Marmont considerably added to their reputations during the campaign.

It was most unfortunate that Napoleon had no one whom he could entrust with the organisation of his armies and was forced to stay in Paris until the last possible moment, for his stroke at Blücher was a few days too late, and though he succeeded in cutting the latter off from the rest of his army, the Prussian general was enabled to effect his junction with the leading corps of the Grand Army. That the Emperor remained so long round La Rothière that he was involved in a general action against a greatly superior force, in a most unfavourable position, was an error which might easily have led to an irretrievable disaster, had it not been for the incompetence of Schwarzenberg. Even as it was the raw French troops were severely shaken and nothing but the almost incredible incapacity and want of energy of their opponents saved the army from annihilation.

His stroke at the flank of the widely dispersed army of Silesia at the beginning of February was most brilliantly carried out, but here again he was favoured by Schwarzenberg's culpable want of energy in failing to maintain touch with a defeated enemy and negligence in not informing Blücher that he had withdrawn the connecting detachment between the two armies.

That Napoleon greatly overrated the effects of the reverse he had inflicted on Blücher cannot be denied, but he had good grounds for his miscalculation, for the way in which the scattered corps of the army of Silesia recovered from their defeat was one of the finest of their many notable achievements during the campaign and spoke well for the spirit of both the leader and his troops. Napoleon's forced march to interpose between Paris and the leading corps of the Grand Army and the manner in which he drove them across the Seine was another brilliantly executed manœuvre, that was crowned with complete success.

Believing that he had crippled the army of Silesia much more severely than was really the case, the Emperor was entirely unprepared for Blücher's rapid advance towards Paris at the end of February, and consequently wasted two or three days at Troyes before he took up the pursuit, but when once he realised the situation, he made a magnificent forced march, but was too late to bring his opponents to action before they crossed the Marne.

He was again delayed by the want of a bridging train, and was once more at fault as to the direction of Blücher's march, for he imagined that the latter was making for Reims, on his way to Chalons, and consequently moved off towards Fismes to intercept him. Thus Blücher was enabled to cross the Aisne practically unmolested, and though the capture of Soissons considerably simplified the operation, the escape of the army of Silesia was really due to Napoleon's erroneous idea of its objective.

When once Blücher had succeeded in effecting his junction with Bulow and Winzingerode, he was too strong to be attacked with impunity, but Napoleon now consistently refused to recognise facts which did not square with his wishes, and persuaded himself that the army of Silesia was retreating northward in disorder. As a matter of fact, Blücher, now that he had succeeded in picking up his reinforcements, was determined to fight at the earliest opportunity, and it was only Winzingerode's lethargy, coupled with some inexcusably bad staff work, that prevented a disaster to the French arms at Craone.

Still blindly adhering to his entirely erroneous belief, and insisting that Laon was only held by a comparatively weak rearguard, Napoleon made a most ill-judged attack on the strong hostile position round the latter town, and was only saved from disaster by Blücher's physical collapse.

The Emperor's bold front on the morning of the 10th of March completely deceived Gneisenau, who had now assumed command of the army of Silesia, causing him to remain on the defensive and countermand the pursuit of Marmont.

It was a desperate move, however, and, had it not been for Blücher's dangerous illness, would probably have entailed an irretrievable disaster.

It was a curious fact that Gneisenau, who had always resented the fact that he had not been entrusted with the supreme command, should have shown himself so absolutely unfitted for it when it was thrust upon him by an accident.

His position, no doubt, was an extremely difficult one, but still it is undeniable that he displayed a great want of firmness in countermanding Blücher's orders for the pursuit of Marmont, in spite of Yorck's and Kleist's urgent remonstrances.

Probably the Emperor would have been far wiser not to have continued his pursuit across the Aisne but to have reoccupied Soissons, left a strong detachment to contain the army of Silesia and have fallen back to the neighbourhood of Meaux, where he would have been in a position to check the advance of either of the hostile armies. His plan of marching into the Rhine provinces, where supplies were still plentiful, and concentrating the garrisons of the frontier fortresses for a determined stroke at Schwarzenberg's communications, had much to recommend it from a purely military point of view.

It had one fatal drawback, however, for Paris would have been unable to hold out until the Emperor's stroke had produced its effect and the occupation of the capital by the Allies would have entailed the immediate collapse of the Napoleonic dynasty.

Taking into consideration the fact that the French troops were seriously demoralised by their heavy losses at both Craone and Laon, the boldly planned and brilliantly carried out stroke at St Priest's corps was a most remarkable achievement, and by his recapture of Reims the Emperor, to a great extent, regained the ground he had lost by the failure of his operations against Blücher. Gneisenau's inaction gave him an opportunity of falling on the flank and rear of the Grand Army, of which he promptly availed himself, and which fulfilled his expectations by throwing Schwarzenberg into a state of panic, checking his operations against Macdonald and causing him to concentrate round Troyes, preparatory to retreating to the Aube.

Had Napoleon moved direct through Arcis on Troyes, instead of marching to his right to Plancy to facilitate his junction with Macdonald, he would probably have burst into the centre of the Grand Army before it had completed its concentration and dealt it a shattering blow.

The Emperor's plan was to call in Macdonald and hasten Schwarzenberg's retreat by marching up both banks of the Aube to Arcis. He then intended to move towards Vitry, where he hoped to be joined by Marmont and Mortier, as well as the garrisons from the fortresses. He would then have some 80,000 men, and adopting a line of communication through Sezanne, he intended to drive Schwarzenberg back to the Rhine, after which he could return to deal with Blücher. Up to a certain point, his calculations proved correct, but Schwarzenberg's decision to discontinue his retreat, and assume the offensive, upset all the Emperor's plans, the more so as such a resolute action on the part of the Austrian generalissimo was entirely unexpected.

In spite of the reports of the country people, Napoleon absolutely refused to believe that Wrede's corps, south of Arcis, was anything but a flank guard covering the retreat of the main body. Hence he became involved in an entirely unpremeditated engagement with the whole of the Allied force, and

was only saved from disaster by his own skill, com·
bined with Schwarzenberg's overcaution and complete inability to handle a large force effectively on
the field of battle.   His retreat to Vitry and decision
to act against his opponent's communications has
often been severely criticised, but though it was
undoubtedly a desperate move, it at least offered
some prospect of drawing the Grand Army away
from Paris, and would probably have achieved its
object had not the dispatch from Savary fallen into
the hands of the Allies.   Its best chance of success
lay in the fact that Blücher, though slowly recover-
ing, had by no means regained his former vigour,
for had the Prussian marshal been in his usual health
the army of Silesia would never have remained in-
active around Laon but would have been well on its
way to Paris.

Napoleon was fully justified in believing that his
success in cutting Schwarzenberg's communications
through Langres to the Rhine would have produced
a much greater effect than it did, but the Austrian
general evinced little concern, as he was prepared
to open up an alternative line through Belgium.

Had the Allies carried out their original intention
of pursuing Napoleon with both the Army of Silesia
and the Grand Army, the Emperor, moving through
St Dizier and Bar-sur-Aube to Troyes, would have

been in a position to check their advance towards Paris, and the situation would have been very much what it was at the beginning of February. The Czar's momentous decision to advance direct on the French capital with the whole available force of the Allies was the death-blow to Napoleon's hopes, and rendered his downfall inevitable. Marmont and Mortier were much too weak even to retard the advance of the Allies and narrowly escaped destruction at Fere Champenoise, when, totally ignorant of the real condition of affairs, they blundered into the midst of the hostile force. Throughout the short campaign, the Emperor had effected some most brilliant *coups* but had never had sufficient strength to follow up his successes, and during the operations following his failure to crush Blücher, before the latter could join Bulow and Winzingerode, there were several occasions on which his actions appear to have been dictated by the recklessness of the gambler rather than the well-considered boldness of the great commander.

The French troops, veterans and conscripts alike, fought with the greatest gallantry, and though they occasionally lost heart and numbers of conscripts strayed from the colours, it must be remembered that the struggle was carried on against hopeless odds, during an exceptionally severe winter.

Of the Allied troops, the Russian veterans appeared to be insensible to hardship or danger, while the Prussians were rendered doubly formidable by their intense patriotism and grim determination to revenge their wrongs, and the contingents of the other states were for the most part composed of seasoned soldiers.

Until towards the end of the campaign, Schwarzenberg appeared in a most unfavourable light, but it must, in common fairness, be admitted that his position was a singularly difficult one, and only a Marlborough or a Wellington could have dealt with it successfully.

The Austrian general was neither a fool nor a traitor, but merely a gallant and honourable gentleman, thrust by fate into a position which he was little qualified to hold. But if Schwarzenberg was over-cautious, it must be admitted that Blücher was somewhat rash, for he displayed a strange want of appreciation of the marvellous ability of his great opponent and was somewhat obsessed by the idea of an immediate advance on the hostile capital, at all costs. But throughout the campaign he displayed an infinitely truer insight as to the military situation than his colleague, and it is impossible to overestimate the advantage derived from his sound common-sense, undaunted courage and cheerful optimism. The Czar was also a tower of strength to the Allies, and his unwavering determination to crush Napoleon went far to neutralise the effects of Schwarzenberg's timidity and the selfish policy of Metternich. The Allies never seemed to realise the danger of dispersion when opposed to such a master of the art of war as Napoleon, and time after time afforded him an opportunity of falling on isolated corps, though they were invariably immensely superior in strength in the theatre of operations.

Their failing was to a great extent due to the misuse of the formidable force of mounted troops, which should at least have rendered them safe from all risk of surprise.

Great Britain played an important part in the campaign, for besides paying large subsidies, which alone enabled her Allies to keep their armies in the field, she had some 60,000 troops under arms in the south of France, Catalonia and the Netherlands. Her main object in continuing the struggle was to force Napoleon to relinquish the formidable fortified harbour of Antwerp, where the remnant of his battle fleet had taken refuge, and which, as long as it remained in French hands, was a standing menace to England's naval supremacy. The Emperor absolutely refused to give up either Antwerp or Genoa, and it was his refusal to relinquish either of the

P

formidable naval bases which rendered an agreement impossible.

That it was the vital issue of an unassailable naval supremacy, and no vulgar lust of conquest, which led Great Britain to continue the struggle is clearly shown by the instructions issued to Lord Castlereagh prior to his setting out to join the headquarters of the Allied army.

At a Cabinet Council held just before Christmas, 1813, he was instructed that " If the maritime power of France shall be restricted within due bounds by the effectual establishment of Holland, the Peninsula and Italy in security and independence, Great Britain, consistent with her own security, may then be inclined to apply the greater portion of her conquests to promote the general interests. If, on the contrary, the arrangements should be defective on any of these points, Great Britain must preserve a proportionate share of these conquests to render her secure against France.

The most important stipulations were " the absolute exclusion of France from any naval establishment on the Scheldt, especially at Antwerp " and " the security of Holland by a barrier including at least Antwerp, Juliers and Maestricht." Under these conditions, Great Britain was prepared to restore to the Dutch the colonies she had captured from them, with the exception of the Cape of Good Hope. The possession of the latter was held to be essential to secure uninterrupted communication with India, but Great Britain was willing to indemnify Holland for its loss, by a payment of £2,000,000, provided that the whole of the sum was expended in strengthening the barrier fortresses.

APPENDIX

IT is extremely difficult to estimate with any degree of accuracy the exact number of troops with which the Allies actually commenced their invasion of France and Belgium in January 1814.

The various authorities differ considerably as to the numbers and composition of the Allied armies; however, it is certain that the whole of Kleist's and the greater part of Langeron's corps were at first engaged in the blockade of Mainz and other fortresses, only joining Blücher at a later stage of the campaign.

General Von Horsetky gives the following as the strength and composition of the Allied forces at the end of 1813, actually on the Rhine and prepared for an immediate advance, and it appears that his figures may be regarded as reasonably accurate.

THE GRAND ARMY (THE ARMY OF BOHEMIA)
Commander—Prince Schwarzenberg
Chief of the Staff—Field-Marshal Radetzky

1st Austrian Corps—Count Colloredo	15,000
2nd Austrian Corps—Prince A. Lichtenstein	15,000

3rd Austrian Corps—General Gyulai   .   15,000
4th Wurtemberg Corps—Prince of Wur-
    temberg   12,000
5th Bavarian Corps—General Wrede   .   35,000
6th Russian Corps—General Wittgenstein   20,000
The Austro-German Corps—General Bianchi   13,000
1st Austrian Light Division—Count Bubna   7,000
2nd Austrian Light Division—Prince M.
    Lichtenstein   4,000
The Austrian Reserve—The Prince of
    Hesse-Homburg   20,000
The Russian Reserve—Marshal Barclay de
    Tolley   35,000

The latter included both the Russian and Prussian Guard, as well as Platoff's Cossacks.

The total force was, roughly, just over 200,000 men and nearly 700 guns.

THE ARMY OF SILESIA

Commander—Field-Marshal Blücher

Chief of the Staff—General Gneisenau

1st Prussian Corps—General Yorck .   .   20,000
2nd Prussian Corps—General Kleist   .   20,000
The Russian Corps of Count Langeron   .   35,000
The Russian Corps of General Sacken   .   20,000

Roughly, 95,000 men and about 450 guns; however, none of Kleist's corps and only just over 7000 of Langeron's corps actually took part in Blücher's advance, so that his strength was in reality only some 50,000 men with 300 guns at the commencement of the campaign.

This would make the united armies about 250,000 strong, with over 1000 guns, and is probably not far from their actual strength.

Of the Army of the North, nominally under the command of Bernadotte, the only troops which were ready to take the field at the commencement of hostilities, were :

The 3rd Prussian Corps—General Bulow . 30,000
The Russian Corps—General Winzingerode 40,000

The British contingent, under Sir Thomas Graham, only took part in the abortive attacks on Antwerp and Bergen-op-Zoom, so cannot be said to have formed part of the field army.

During the campaign, the following reinforcements joined the Allies in France :

For the Grand Army, during February :

A Russian Division 9,000
A Wurtemberg Division 10,500
The 8th German Corps 10,300

For the Army of Silesia, during February and March :

Kleist's Corps 9,000
Langeron's Corps 10,000

Bulow and Winzingerode's corps also joined Blücher at the beginning of March, but their strength had been considerably reduced by detachments left to hold the fortresses on the lines of communications.

Saxe-Weimar's corps, consisting of troops furnished by the smaller German states, was left to carry on field operations and succeeded in forcing General Maison back to the line of fortresses guarding the French frontier but was unable to achieve anything further.

Wellington's army in the south of France consisted of, roughly, 100,000 men, being composed as follows :—

British and King's German Legion . .	46,000
Portuguese	24,000
Spaniards	30,000

So that, in all, the Allied forces employed in France between the 1st of January and the 31st of March 1814 amounted to the formidable total of about 450,000 men.

Owing to the disasters and enormous losses of the campaigns of 1812 and 1813, the organisation of permanent corps, under selected commanders, which had been in force in the French army for some ten years, had to a great extent ceased to exist.

Divisions and brigades were usually so much under strength, and fluctuated so considerably in numbers at different periods of the campaign, that these titles almost entirely lost their significance.

Most of the authorities agree that the strength of the field army under Napoleon's immediate command at the commencement of the campaign was, roughly, 100,000 men and 300 guns.

In the south of France, Soult probably had about 60,000 men available for operations in the field, while the garrisons of Bayonne, St Jean Pied-de-Port and other small fortresses certainly did not amount to over 10,000 men.

There were also a few thousand regular troops round Lyons and in the valley of the Rhone, which were afterwards reinforced by strong drafts from the forces under Soult and Suchet, to form the Army of the South, commanded by Augereau. The garrisons of the various fortresses on the northern and eastern frontier of France may, perhaps, have amounted to a little over 50,000 men, the bulk of whom were in Mainz, Metz, Thionville, Luxemburg and Strassburg.

So that at the commencement of the year, the Emperor can have had little more than 200,000 men, including garrison troops, in the various theatres of operations.

At the end of January the Emperor had, actually available for field operations, only some 70,000 men, distributed as follows.

1. Round Chalons—

Victor, with Milhaud's cavalry, between
Vitry and St Dizier   15,000
Marmont, with Doumerc's cavalry, east
of Chalons   12,000
Ney, with Lefebvre-Desnouettes' cavalry
at Chalons   14,500

2. Round Troyes, under Mortier—

The Old Guard and Reserve Corps   .   20,000

3. On the march from Mezières to St
Menhould, under Macdonald   .   .   10,000

These latter troops, though they formed the extreme left of the French field army, were not available for immediate operations and took no part in the Emperor's first offensive movement, but were engaged with Yorck's corps of the army of Silesia in the valley of the Marne.

During the campaign he received large drafts of conscripts from the interior of France, but it is almost impossible to ascertain even their approximate number, as the Emperor consistently overestimated the numbers joining the army during the first few weeks of the campaign, in order to reassure the country and impose upon the Allies.

Soult's army also received a large number of recruits during January, but this was more than balanced by the strong drafts of veterans he was ordered to send to the Emperor.

A most notable feature of the campaign was the magnificent way in which the immature and untrained conscripts fought, when animated by the presence of the Emperor, who had lost none of his marvellous power of stirring the hearts of his soldiery.

In his " Napoleon and the Campaign of 1814," Houssaye pays a glowing but, on the whole, thoroughly well-deserved tribute to the courage and endurance of these lads.

One thing, unfortunately, which is not open to doubt is the lamentable condition of the recruits on their arrival at the main depot of Courbevoie, on the western outskirts of Paris. The conscripts were often without food or accommodation, and it was useless to complain to the overworked officers of the depot, who lost their heads among the crowds of recruits waiting to be organised and lacking every necessary.

In spite of all deficiencies, of the 50,000 conscripts who passed through the depot of Courbevoie in the

space of three months, only one per cent. deserted.
What a testimony to the honour of the soldiers of
1814 ! These poor youths, whose eyes filled with
tears as they were dragged away from their desolate
homes, were quickly transformed by the sight of the
colours.

From the bronzed veterans who had conquered
Europe, they learnt the noble self-denial and the
cheerful fatalism which form the basis of the military
spirit, and then one day, at a review or before a
battle, the Emperor passed before them and they
came under the spell of his fascination ; from that
moment they fought not from a sense of duty, not
from patriotism, but solely for Napoleon.

The nickname of " Marie-Louises " was given to
these poor little soldiers who had been hurriedly
torn from their homes and formed into regiments,
and a fortnight later were hurled into the thick of
the battle, and this name of " Marie-Louise " they
wrote large in their blood across the page of history.

Those cuirassiers who could hardly sit their horses
and whose furious charge crushed five hostile
squadrons at Valjouan, they were " Marie-Louises."

Those cavalry were " Marie-Louises " of whom
General Delort said : " No one but a madman would
expect me to charge with such cavalry," and who
burst through Montereau like a flood, overwhelming

the Austrian battalions massed in the streets. It was a "Marie-Louise" who stood in his place immovable under a heavy fire, alike indifferent to the noise of the bullets and the sight of the men struck down beside him, and who answered Marshal Marmont: "I would fire as much as anyone else, only I don't know how to load my musket."

It was a "Marie-Louise" who took General Oolsofief prisoner at Champaubert and would hand him over to none but the Emperor himself.

At Bar-sur-Aube and Craone they again proved their constancy, facing enormous losses with unflinching courage, while at Fere-Champenoise, without hope of support, they stood at bay and for some time beat off the attacks of the overwhelming force of the magnificent Russian and Prussian cavalry, supported by a formidable array of horse artillery.

The "Marie-Louises" went coatless in the bitter frost; ill-clad and ill-fed they tramped bare-footed through the snow, they scarcely knew how to use their weapons, and day after day they fought stern and bloody battles.

Yet through the whole campaign they uttered no word of complaint, and in the ranks there was no murmur against the Emperor.

Truly France has the right to feel proud of her "Marie-Louises."

Besides these heroic conscripts, there was the National Guard, composed of men either too young or too old to be taken as recruits, but with the exception of the battalions raised in Paris, they were almost entirely lacking in organisation, training or equipment and cannot be held in any sense to have been an efficient military force.

LIST OF THE PRINCIPAL AUTHORITIES CONSULTED

Alison's " History of Europe."

General Sir E. B. Hamley's " Operations of War."

General Von Horsetzky's " Chief Campaigns in Europe, since 1792."

Field-Marshal Viscount Wolseley's " Decline and Fall of Napoleon."

Napier's " History of the War in the Peninsula and the South of France."

H. Houssaye's " Napoleon and the Campaign of 1814."

Mr F. Lorraine Petre's " Napoleon at Bay, 1814."

" Blücher," The Heroes of the Nations Series, by Mr E. F. Henderson.

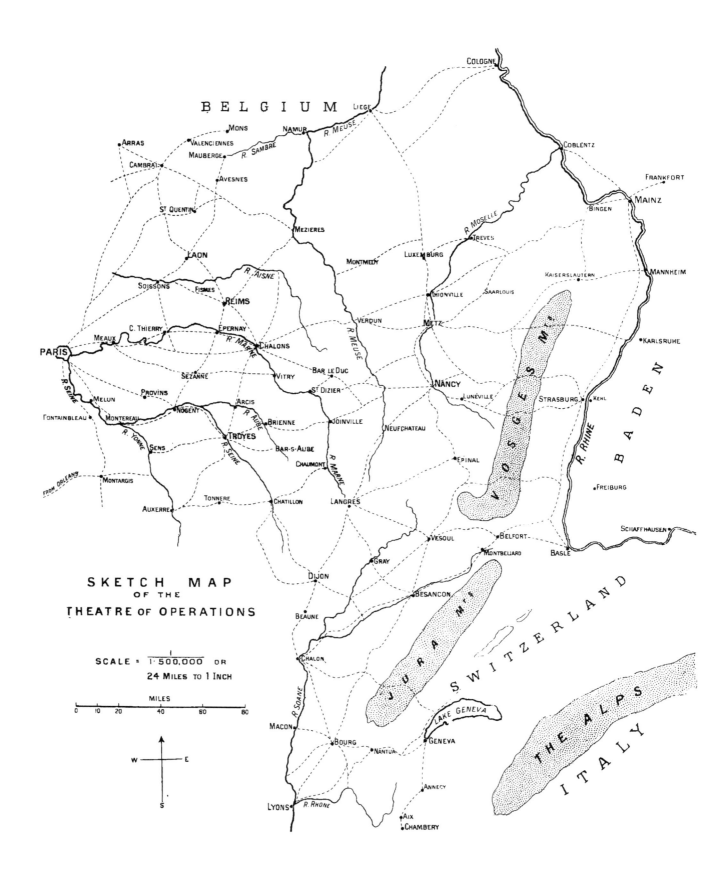

BELGIUM

MONS
ARRAS
VALENCIENNES
NAMUR
R. MEUSE
LIEGE
COLOGNE
MAUBERGE
R. SAMBRE
COBLENTZ
CAMBRAI
AVESNES
FRANKFORT
ST QUENTIN
MEZIERES
MAINZ
BINGEN
LAON
R. AISNE
MONTMEDY
LUXEMBURG
TREVES
R. MOSELLE
MANNHEIM
SOISSONS
FISMES
REIMS
KAISERSLAUTERN
C. THIERRY
EPERNAY
VERDUN
THIONVILLE
SAARLOUIS
PARIS
MEAUX
R. MARNE
CHALONS
R. MEUSE
METZ
KARLSRUHE
SEZANNE
VITRY
BAR LE DUC
BADEN
MELUN
PROVINS
ARCIS
ST DIZIER
NANCY
STRASBURG
KEHL
FONTAINBLEAU
MONTEREAU
NOGENT
R. AUBE
BRIENNE
JOINVILLE
LUNÉVILLE
R. RHINE
R. SEINE
TROYES
BAR-S-AUBE
NEUFCHATEAU
R. YONNE
SENS
R. SEINE
CHAUMONT
R. MARNE
EPINAL
FREIBURG
FROM ORLEANS
MONTARGIS
TONNERE
CHATILLON
LANGRES
VOSGES M.
AUXERRE
VESOUL
BELFORT
SCHAFFHAUSEN
GRAY
MONTBELIARD
BASLE
DIJON
BEAUNE
BESANCON
R. SOARNE
CHALON
JURA M.
SWITZERLAND
THE ALPS
ITALY
MACON
BOURG
NANTUA
LAKE GENEVA
GENEVA
ANNECY
LYONS
R. RHONE
AIX
CHAMBERY

SKETCH MAP
OF THE
THEATRE OF OPERATIONS

SCALE = $\frac{1}{1.500,000}$ OR
24 MILES TO 1 INCH

MILES
0   10   20   40   60   80

W —|— E
S

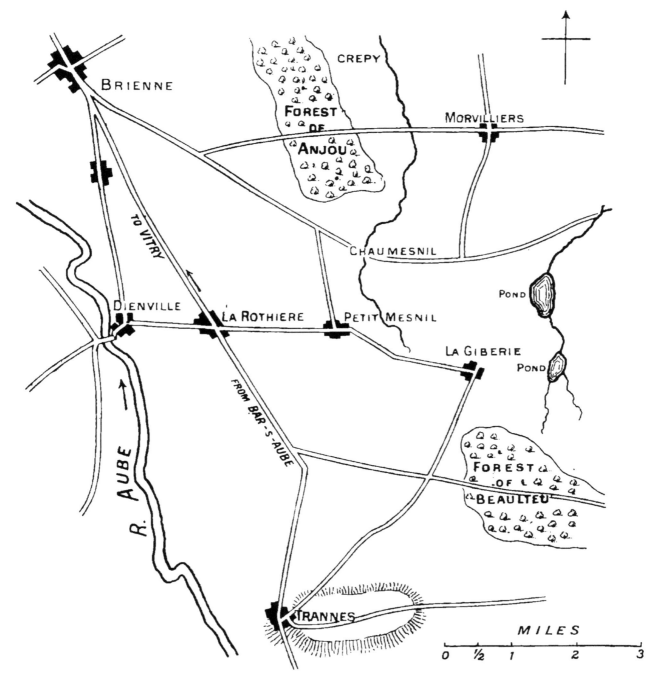

SKETCH PLAN OF THE BATTLE FIELD OF LA ROTHIERE

BRIENNE

CREPY

FOREST OF ANJOU

MORVILLIERS

TO VITRY

CHAUMESNIL

DIENVILLE

LA ROTHIERE

PETIT MESNIL

POND

LA GIBERIE

POND

FROM BAR-S-AUBE

R. AUBE

FOREST OF BEAULIEU

TRANNES

MILES

0   ½   1   2   3

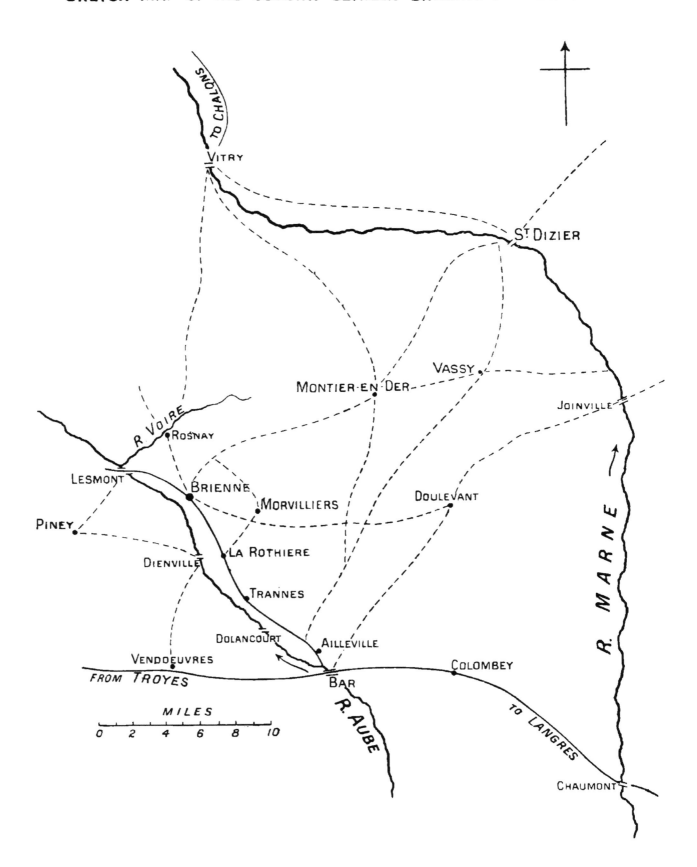

SKETCH MAP OF THE COUNTRY BETWEEN BRIENNE & ST DIZIER

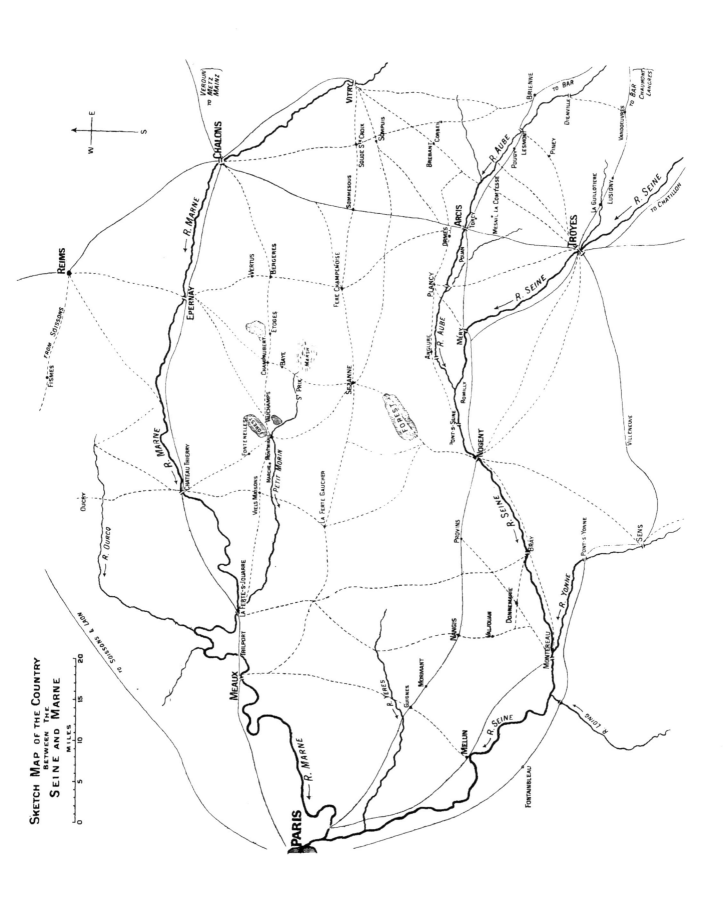

SKETCH MAP OF THE COUNTRY
BETWEEN THE
SEINE AND MARNE

MILES

0   5   10   15   20

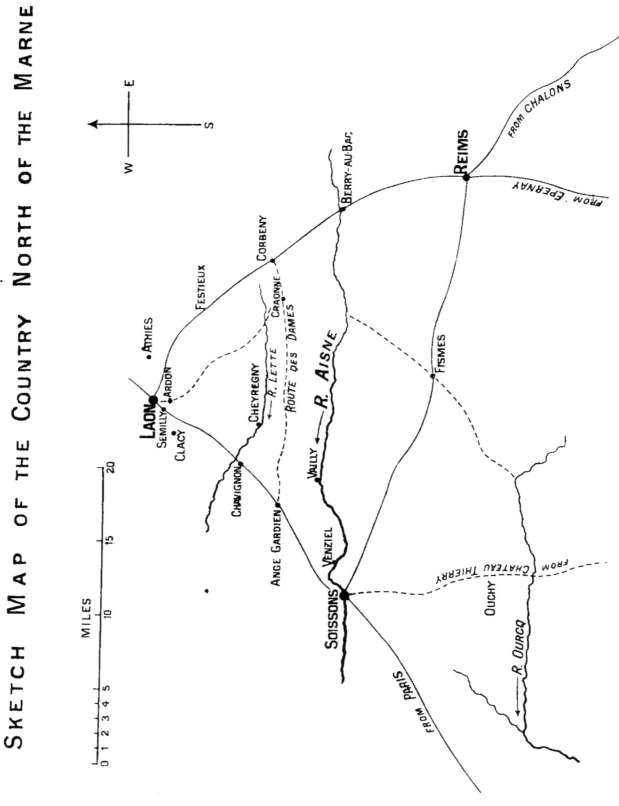

SKETCH MAP OF THE COUNTRY NORTH OF THE MARNE

MILES
0 1 2 3 4 5   10   15   20

W   E
S

FROM CHALONS

REIMS

FROM EPERNAY

BERRY-AU-BAC.

CORBENY

FESTIEUX

ATHIES

FISMES

LAON
SEMILLY ARDON
CLACY

CHEYREGNY
CRAONNE
R. LETTE
ROUTE DES DAMES

R. AISNE

CHAVIGNON

ANGE GARDIEN

VAILLY

VENZIEL

SOISSONS

FROM CHATEAU THIERRY

OUCHY

R. OURCQ

FROM PARIS

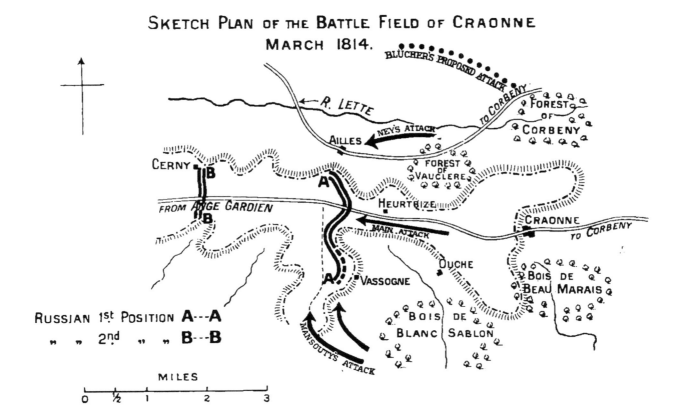

SKETCH PLAN OF THE BATTLE FIELD OF CRAONNE
MARCH 1814.

BLÜCHER'S PROPOSED ATTACK

R. LETTE

TO CORBENY

FOREST OF CORBENY

NEY'S ATTACK

AILLES

FOREST OF VAUCLERE

CERNY

B

A

HEURTBIZE

CRAONNE

TO CORBENY

FROM ANGE GARDIEN

B

MAIN ATTACK

A

OUCHE

BOIS DE BEAU MARAIS

VASSOGNE

BOIS DE BLANC SABLON

MANSOUTY'S ATTACK

RUSSIAN 1st POSITION A---A

" " 2nd " " B---B

MILES

0   ½   1   2   3

SKETCH PLAN OF THE BATTLE FIELD OF LAON
MARCH 1814.

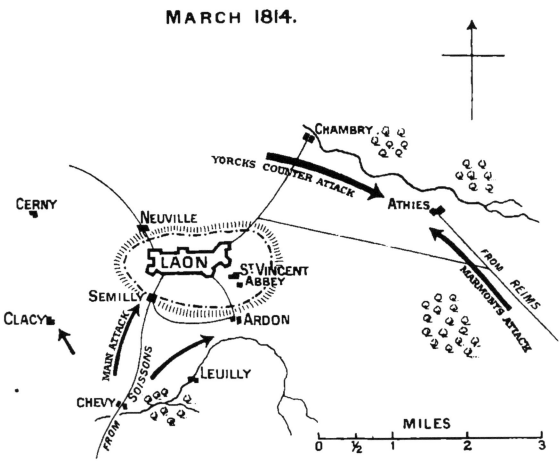

CHAMBRY

YORCKS COUNTER ATTACK

CERNY

NEUVILLE

ATHIES

LAON

St VINCENT ABBEY

FROM REIMS

SEMILLY

MARMONTS ATTACK

CLACY

MAIN ATTACK

ARDON

FROM SOISSONS

LEUILLY

CHEVY

MILES

0   ½   1   2   3

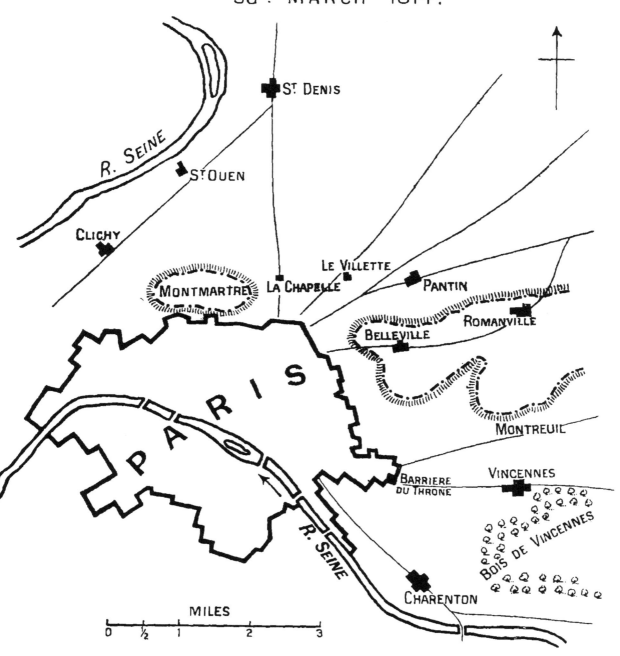

THE ENVIRONS OF PARIS (EASTERN)
30TH MARCH 1814.

Sketch Plan of the Battle Field of Arcis-sur-Aube 20-21st March 1814.

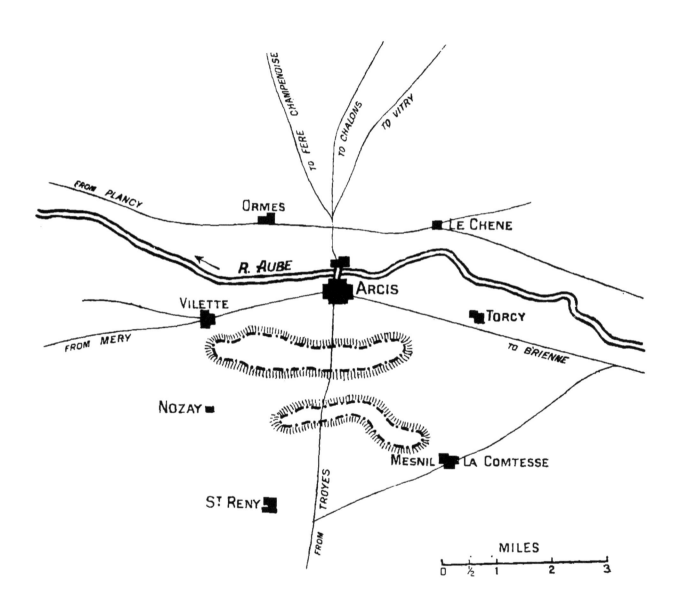

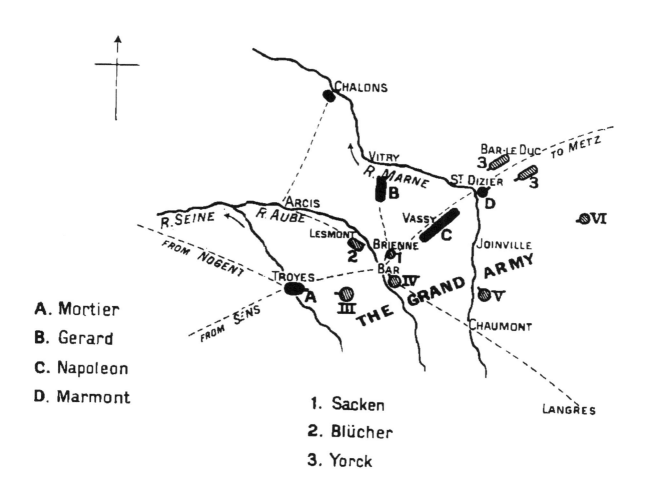

POSITIONS OF THE FRENCH AND ALLIES
28TH JANUARY 1814.

A

CHALONS

VITRY

R. MARNE

BAR-LE-DUC — TO METZ

3

ST. DIZIER

B

D

ARCIS

R. SEINE

R. AUBE

VASSY

VI

LESMONT

BRIENNE

C

2

JOINVILLE

FROM NOGENT

BAR

1

TROYES

IV

ARMY

FROM SENS

A

III

V

THE GRAND

CHAUMONT

LANGRES

A. Mortier
B. Gerard
C. Napoleon
D. Marmont

1. Sacken
2. Blücher
3. Yorck

POSITIONS OF THE FRENCH AND ALLIES
9TH FEBRUARY 1814.

B

LA FERTE-S-JOUARRE

CHATEAU THIERRY

R. MARNE

MEAUX

PARIS

C

2

1

THE ARMY OF SILESIA

H.Q.

CHALONS

3

4

SEZANNE

A

B

NOGENT

R. SEINE

R. SEINE

ARCIS

R. AUBE

MONTEREAU

VI

R. YONNE

THE GRAND ARMY

BAR

TROYES

GUARD
RESERVE

SENS

IV

III

I

A. Napoleon

B.

C. Macdonald

1. Sacken

2. Yorck

3. Kleist   4. Oolsofief

POSITIONS OF THE FRENCH AND ALLIES 16TH FEBRUARY 1814.

C

R. MARNE

MEAUX
B
MONTMIRAIL
A
CHALONS
THE ARMY OF SILESIA

PARIS
C
D
R. SEINE
VI V
R. SEINE
NOGENT
GUARD
ARCIS
R. AUBE

FONTAINBLEAU
MONTEREAU
BRAY
I IV
THE GRAND ARMY
R. SEINE
TROYES

R. YONNE
SENS
RESERVE

A. Marmont

B. Grouchy

C. Napoleon

D. Victor

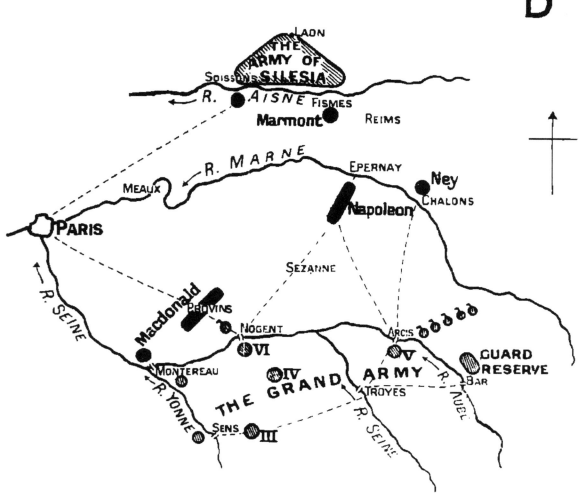

POSITIONS OF THE FRENCH AND ALLIES 17TH MARCH 1814.

D